A HISTORY OF IRELAND IN 100 OBJECTS

A HISTORY OF
IRELAND IN
100 OBJECTS

Fintan O'Toole
The Irish Times

RIA

A History of Ireland in 100 Objects

First published 2013
by Royal Irish Academy.
19 Dawson Street
Dublin 2

www.ria.ie

This is a project of

THE IRISH TIMES

ISBN 978-1-908996-15-2

Copyeditor: Helena King
Project Coordinator: Pauline McNamara
Digital Specialist: Geoffrey Keating
Design: Fidelma Slattery
Academic Mentor: Peter Harbison
Index: Helen Litton

Printed in Spain by Estudios Gráficos Zure

10 9 8 7 6 5 4 3 2 1

INTRODUCTION
FINTAN O'TOOLE

Even the most perfect reproduction of a work…is lacking in one element: its presence in time and space, its unique existence at the place where it happens to be.

Walter Benjamin

I

The story of human beings on the island of Ireland is very short. The earliest evidence of people living here goes back only to c. 8000 BC, to the era known as the Mesolithic or middle stone age. This may seem like a long time, but not when we remember that there may have been people living in southern Britain over a quarter of a million years ago. Early humans, in their gradual expansion out of Africa, moved vast distances across Asia and through the full length of America, but there are no traces of them having made it to Ireland. If any of them did come here as hunters, they would certainly have retreated by around 23,000 years ago, when expanding glaciers and intense cold made north-western Europe inhospitable. When people began to push northwards again around 15,000 years ago, no one seems to have settled in Ireland. Again, even if they did, they would almost certainly have been pushed out by another long period of severe cold around 11000 BC, which killed off many of the animals on which they might have lived, such as the giant Irish elk. This left Ireland with a relatively poor range of large mammals. The earliest Irish settlers, at sites such as Mount Sandel in Co. Derry and Lough Boora in Co. Offaly, seem to have depended heavily on wild boar and fish for their non-plant foods. Ireland was not an easy place in which to survive.

These conditions had two effects. One is that Irish culture is quite a recent and concentrated phenomenon. Most of it still exists, of course, in the long obscurity of prehistory. It is not, however, a vast, panoramic epic— it can be imagined as a single story. The other effect is that, from the beginning, those who settled in Ireland had to adapt to conditions that were not typical of southern or western Europe. The food and the environment were, by the European standards of the time, unusual. As archaeologist J.P. Mallory puts it 'the earliest occupants of Ireland were not merely an extension of their ancestral population, but one that was required to adapt to a very different environment and develop uniquely Irish strategies to survive'.

We do not really know where the first people to settle in Ireland came from. One possibility is an area between north Wales and the Solway Firth on the west coast of Britain that was being gradually inundated by rising sea levels and that is now, indeed, under the Irish Sea. What does seem clear is that, for a very long time, the number of people on the island was very small. For the first 40 per cent of the whole period in which Ireland has been occupied, the total population was probably of the order of 3,000 people. This gives us a third significant aspect of the emerging story of Ireland: it was small. We have, then, three characteristics present from the beginning of Irish culture: concentrated in time, shaped by distinctive conditions and small in scale.

This is not to suggest that Ireland was a place apart, or that its culture was not transformed from time to time by incoming people and new developments. Easily the biggest of such developments was the arrival of farming around 4000

BC. We know that this cannot have been simply a spontaneous discovery by the people who already inhabited the island. Ireland did not have wild cereals or wild cattle, sheep or goats that could be domesticated—they had to come from somewhere else. New kinds of houses and pottery and the emergence of great passage tombs came with the development of farming, making it likely that the first farmers arrived from elsewhere—most probably Britain or (less likely) north-western France.

Other big changes tended to happen in the same way. The emergence of metal-working (around 2500 BC) was probably the result of some inward migration of so-called Beaker people from Britain and continental Europe. The development of an elite warrior culture about a thousand years later seems to be associated with the presence of at least some foreigners from as far away as central Europe, and is certainly linked to intense contacts with Britain and the continent. (Ironically, one of the 'invasions' for which there is no evidence at all is that most famously associated with Ireland—the supposed arrival of the Celts.) Contacts such as these are probably also at the root of the development of the early forms of language that emerged in Ireland, which may have evolved as a *lingua franca* for Atlantic Europe.

Other huge changes also came from outside. Christianity brought a new belief system, literacy, the learning of the Graeco-Roman and Jewish worlds and entry into a 'universal' culture. The Vikings brought urban settlements and money. The Anglo-Normans brought feudalism. The English brought cities, a new language, printing, new systems of administration and land management and the end of clan power. The European

Union enabled rapid urbanisation and 'modernity'. Corporations based in the United States brought economic globalisation and technological transformation.

Yet, these waves of change always washed up on the same shores. Even the most profound influences are continually adapted to what is there already. There is a continuity of population—surveys of Ireland's genetic profile fail to find any significant evidence of large-scale inward migrations after those of the early farmers. Moreover, there is also a cultural continuity. It is not static, not a fixed inheritance of images and ideas that is passed on from time immemorial. It is, rather, a way of using the old to make sense of the new. From very early on, the people living in Ireland make objects that suit themselves and their own conditions: even the very early stone tools found in Ireland are distinctive. Throughout Irish history, this remains true. The place—its geography and environment, its particular mixture of 'native' and 'foreigner' (categories that change radically over time)—exerts its own peculiar pressures. People respond to those pressures as best they can, trying to adapt to change while taking comfort in what is familiar.

This is as true of the latest objects featured in this selection as it is of the earliest. It may be the case that globalisation spreads the same objects everywhere, and we can certainly see this happening in Ireland. Nevertheless, it is striking that even our final object is an international product that has been adapted for a very specific Irish purpose: the Russian-designed AK47 assault rifle that has been adapted to Irish needs by making it impossible to use. Even now, the three features of Irish culture present from the start—concentrated, distinctive and small—still apply.

II

But why tell this story through physical objects? Does a physical object, in our digital age, still mean anything? With the technologies at our disposal, almost any object can be reproduced with absolute precision. Worn or smudged surfaces can be turned into clear and vibrant images. Fragments can be recast as unified entities. Reproductions can have the same feel and form as the original. They can even surpass it—the detail we can see in contemporary prints from the *Book of Kells* goes well beyond what was visible to most of those who handled the real thing. Some people who run museums have concluded that in the digital age, we are no longer interested in mere inert *things* and must be immersed in *experiences*.

There is plenty of good theory to justify this belief. Why should we make a fetish of an object just because it is old? Why should we imagine that the idea of an original means anything in a culture of mass reproduction? After all, the making of multiple copies of an object has been possible for a long time—the ancient Greeks made bronzes, terracotta and coins in this way. Are they less beautiful because they are not 'original'? The development of woodcuts, engraving, etching and printing long ago blurred the line between the original and the copy.

Is there not something primitive, or on the other hand something unhealthily consumerist, about treating objects with reverence? Is there any real difference between the desire to see the original of, say the *Book of Kells*, and the creepy compulsion that makes someone pay a year's salary to buy one of Elvis Presley's used hankies on eBay?

There is a good, sober, respectably scientific answer to these questions. Unlike reproductions or digital images, original objects are not static. They contain secrets that can be unlocked with ever newer techniques. We are learning astonishing things from old objects, things we never thought they could reveal—exactly how old they are, where they came from, what their own histories might be. No-one knew even a few decades ago that it would be possible some day to use tiny fragments of an ancient object to figure out its age, or that the chemicals in the teeth of a body in a grave might tell us where the owner of an ancient sword had spent his youth. Yet, objects can now tell us startling stories—that the stone for an ancient ceremonial axe found in the west of Ireland came from the Alps, or that the man who brought a beautiful gold ornament to these islands grew up thousands of kilometres to the east.

Beyond this eminently rational excuse for being fascinated with original objects there is nevertheless an irrational force. You feel it every time you look at something in a museum, find it interesting, and then, looking at the label, see the words 'this is a copy. The original is...'. There is a deep and entirely unreasonable disappointment. You know that what you are seeing is probably better, clearer, more whole, than the original; it is not, however, the thing itself. That disappointment tells us something important about the magnetic attractiveness of historic objects.

Perhaps life in a digital culture enhances, rather than detracts from, this magnetism. We live with vastly more images than any humans have ever done. James Joyce coined the phrase 'bairdboard bombardment screen' to describe television, but the bombardment of the senses with rapidly-shifting two-dimensional pictures has become almost unavoidable in contemporary urban life. Maybe for this very reason a three-dimensional object that comes to us over the oceans of time has an aura of quiet strangeness. It occupies a different kind of space, and it is, as John Keats called his Grecian urn, the 'foster child of silence and slow time'.

An old object does not carry such a potent charge just because of the things that can be reproduced so well with our technologies—the form, the materials, the decorative skills. Its value does not even lie in the unique information it can impart to archaeologists, historians and scientists. What makes it pulse with life is the idea of the people who touched and were touched by it. It is the hands that made it, the eyes that feasted on or feared it, the terror, wonder or delight it evoked. It is the simple, awe-inspiring thought—this thing connects me to my ancestors. It is, in Walter Benjamin's phrase, 'the history to which it was subject throughout the time of its existence'. I may never fully understand it, especially if it comes from the very distant past, but in the moment I encounter it, I am sharing some tiny fragment of the lives that it touched.

This sense of sharing something with the past is not entirely abstract. Many of the things that survive from the past had an aura of magic about them. Sometimes they were created specifically to generate that feeling of awe. Sometimes they acquired it through their association with momentous events. The magic they have for us may spring from different considerations (that they are old and famous), but it is at least analogous to what our ancestors may have felt in their presence. If you look at a magical jadeitite axe from 6,000 years ago, the feeling you get is still the feeling it was meant to evoke, that of being in the presence of a thing that represents a force beyond the merely physical, something large and mysteriously evocative. The Greeks had a word for it—*charis*, the allure of objects.

Objects can put us in touch with the past in this direct and immediate way, but they also help us to a more complex understanding of that past. There is a certain paradox that surrounds them. They seem precise and fixed, literally tangible. When so much about the past—especially the Irish past—is contested, physical things seem to provide secure anchors in history. They ought to make things simpler. Yet, when you actually examine any object, this apparent simplicity quickly falls away.

Interesting objects tend to provoke more questions than they can answer. There are the simple questions: why and when were they made? How were they used? These often turn out to be not quite so simple, especially with objects of great antiquity. In the case of Ireland, where much of prehistory is still obscure, early objects sometimes serve to tell us how much we do not yet know. They give us glimpses of a tangible certainty, only to keep it beyond our grasp.

Beyond the basic questions, there is always the larger one: what did this thing *mean* when it was made? As the dates come closer to our own, it becomes easier to attempt an answer, because the culture becomes more like our own and we have so much more information. The further we reach back in time, however, the more we are reminded of the inescapable fact that an object is mute without its context. Whether it is a silver candlestick from Georgian Dublin or an illuminated page of the *Book of Kells*, a conical button from Viking Ireland or a gold disc from the Bronze Age, an Eileen Gray chair or a Stone Age macehead from Knowth, it carries its own codes of meaning. It expresses some kind of power—religious, political or economic. It suggests a place in the world—that of its owner and that of those it was intended to impress. Objects do not just *have* stories, they *tell* stories. What they said to their contemporaries may, however, be very different from what they now say to us.

For this very reason, historians would tend to be sceptical of the very idea of a history of Ireland in 100 objects. History is based above all on documents—the written word reveals not just actions but intentions. Texts open up contexts. Mere objects, on the other hand, are seldom eloquent in themselves. The fish trap with which we start our selection, for example, is an amazing thing—but only if someone tells you what it is and how extraordinary is its survival. On its own, it looks like a bunch of sticks stuck in a slab of turf.

No one would dispute this. Even archaeologists will stress that the objects they uncover, however beautiful, are of little use without their wider context, a context that is usually provided by the scientist or the historian. Yet there are at least two good reasons for starting with objects and using them to sketch the development of human societies and cultures on this island.

One is that very quality of immediacy that a significant object carries with it. The digital age we inhabit seems to make physical things less important, but it does the same for time and sequence. On the internet, everything seems to exist together simultaneously. The idea of chronology, of the way one thing follows another, is losing its grasp. Objects, so striking in themselves, can be arranged in such a way that the unfolding of change can be experienced tangibly, especially if, as we hope, readers take the opportunity to go and see them for themselves. (Apart from anything else, the National Museum and the other great repositories of striking objects are a great free resource in lean times.)

The other good reason for doing this history of the island through objects has to do with history itself. Ireland, at least as much as any other place, has been awash with grand narratives and epic histories, which all come, of course, in competing versions. The thing about these big narratives, though, is that they tend to fall apart, or at least to get very complicated, when you scale down the field of study. Biography tends to reveal more ambiguities than local histories, and local histories tend to contain more contradictions than national narratives.

For this reason, much of recent Irish history-writing has tended to concentrate on the small scale and the fine detail. This is an admirable reaction against the inadequacy of the grand narratives, but it does leave non-historians feeling somewhat excluded. By unfolding a rough history of Ireland through 100 objects, it is possible to combine the virtues of micro-history (what could be more micro than a single thing?) with a broad chronological narrative. It is possible to tell a 'story of Ireland' that is complex and ambiguous but at the same time broad and engaging.

We have therefore chosen 100 remarkable objects, each of which opens a window onto an important moment in Irish history. Most come from the great trove that is the National Museum, a resource that is itself one of the wonders of Ireland. The rest are from a variety of other institutions. They are not intended to be the 100 most remarkable objects on the island, or even to be a representative sample of the great collections. They are chosen simply for their ability to illuminate moments of change, development or crisis.

We have adopted three simple rules. An 'object' is defined as a single, man-made entity—a definition that does not include buildings; the objects are presented in broad chronological order; and, unless there is an overwhelming case to the contrary, the objects themselves are freely accessible to readers in public institutions or spaces. If nothing else, these fascinating things should act as a reminder that Irish people have been around for a while and have survived ordeals and challenges with creativity, resilience and a remarkable ability to invent new ways to say old things.

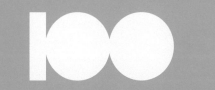

1. MESOLITHIC FISH TRAP, c.5000 BC

It does not look like much: some small, smooth interwoven sticks embedded in the turf from a bog at Clowanstown, in Co. Meath. The bog, however, was once a lake, and the woven sticks are an astonishing survival: part of a conical trap used by early Irish people to scoop fish from the lake or catch them in a weir. Radiocarbon tests date it to between 5210 and 4970 BC. The delicacy of the work has survived the millennia. Nimble hands interlaced young twigs of alder and birch, gathered from the edge of dense woods that covered the land at the time. The warp-and-weft technique is similar to the way of weaving cloth that developed much later in human history. The Irish trap could be called a classic design: similar items continue to be used around the world.

The people who made this trap were adept at using what was around them. They made circular, tent-like huts using saplings; they turned flint and chert stones into knives and other tools, but, as the trap suggests, this was as much an age of wood as of stone. They foraged, hunted and fished, gradually making a human mark on what had been an outpost of untouched nature. In human terms Ireland is a very new country.

Recent finds suggest the movement of our species out of Africa may have begun more than 125,000 years ago. There is evidence of settlement in Britain by people like ourselves as far back as 40,000 years ago, but there is no evidence of human settlement in Ireland before 8000 BC.

When hunter-gatherers did arrive from Britain, they found a densely forested landscape, a temperate climate and an abundance of animals, including wild pigs, wolves and bears (though not yet deer). Brown trout, salmon and eel were abundant in rivers and lakes. It is not accidental that the earliest settlements yet identified in Ireland, at Mount Sandel, in Co. Derry, and Lough Boora, in Co. Offaly, were close to water.

The people who made the Clowanstown trap may have moved with the seasons, following their best sources of food. They would probably not have seen themselves as belonging to a single, large, overarching group. Yet the flint tools they made were gradually becoming distinctive and different from those in Britain. Slowly and unconsciously, Ireland was emerging as a particular human space.

WHERE TO SEE IT: NATIONAL MUSEUM OF IRELAND-ARCHAEOLOGY, KILDARE STREET, DUBLIN 2; 00-353-1-6677444; WWW.MUSEUM.IE

Even now, its shine and colour are magnetically alluring, its green surface, mottled with darker veins and glimmers of light, polished to a glassy sheen. The shape is beautifully balanced between sharp edges and elegant curves. It was once thought that it must have come from China, and if it looks exotic and mysterious now, it would have seemed astonishing nearly 6,000 years ago in Ireland.

The jadeitite axehead, from Kincraigy, Co. Donegal, was never used to cut anything. It was always a rare and precious object, made not only to enhance the prestige of its owner but as a sacred thing in its own right. We now know just how exotic it was: in 2008 analysis revealed that it came from Mont Beigua, high in the Italian Alps near Genoa, over 1,600 km from its final resting place. It required enormous skill to make it, and it was already up to 700 years old when it reached Ireland in 3600 BC.

The axehead tells us two big things. One is that prehistoric objects can have long and complicated life histories, and could travel incredible distances. This object had not travelled directly to Kincraigy from the source, but had circulated around north-west Europe. Its shape was changed and it received its glassy polish at some distance from the Alps, probably in the Paris Basin, some time between 4500 BC and 4000 BC. The people who brought it to Ireland will not have known where the Alps were, but they would have known that the axehead had come from the 'magic mountains', close to the world of the gods, far away. It would have had its own legendary history, perhaps even a name.

The second big thing this object tells us is about agriculture, and the revolutionary changes that brought. Why is this ultra-special object an axehead? Because it was axes that allowed the dense woodlands to be cleared. The axe was the symbol of human power over nature. This piece of Italian exotica points us towards the single biggest transformation in Irish history: the adoption of farming around 4000 BC. This axehead was probably brought to Ireland by immigrant farming groups from northern France—coming either directly, or through Britain, and establishing a tangibly Continental lifestyle on our shores (similar jadeitite axes from Mount Viso in the Italian Alps were being imported into Britain, France, Denmark and Germany). The immigrant farmers would have had to bring their domestic animals and cereals with them, since the wild ancestors of wheat, barley, cattle and sheep did not exist on the island of Ireland. The axehead would have formed part of this package of novelties. It was probably a precious community heirloom, and its owners may have believed it could protect them during their long and dangerous journey. Once in Ireland, it would have been treasured before being deposited in a boggy spot. Mary Cahill of the National Museum believes that the axe may have passed from hand to hand as part of a 'bride price' or dowry. Farming created larger-scale settled communities with a strong sense of territory and ownership, and chieftains rich enough to own a fabulously exotic object.

100 WHERE TO SEE IT: NATIONAL MUSEUM OF IRELAND-ARCHAEOLOGY, KILDARE STREET, DUBLIN 2; 00-353-1-6777444; WWW.MUSEUM.IE

The bowl is simple enough, very dark with burnished surfaces and relatively crude lattice-pattern decorations. It may have been used for drinking, and similar vessels have been found elsewhere in Ireland.

Yet, because of the context in which it was found, this everyday object is extraordinarily eloquent. It tells us a great deal about the lives of some of the earliest Irish farmers. It was discovered in 1992 along with remains of three other pots, in a small cave in Annagh, in the east of Co. Limerick, that contained three full human skeletons, two other sets of partial remains, various animal bones and a flint blade and arrowhead. The bowl and pots tell us that the people were farmers; the other objects tell us that they were also hunters and warriors. Thus, this ancient grave offers two major revelations. One is that the development of agriculture was accompanied by considerable violence. The men who were chosen for burial at Annagh seem to have been veteran local champions or heroes. Two of them were in their 50s when they died—perhaps 20 years older than the norm. All three had suffered violence: two had serious head injuries, one a broken nose, one a fractured rib. In one case, the blow to the skull was delivered with such force that it must have been inflicted by something like a slingshot. Beside the plain domesticity of the bowl, there are the vestiges of brutal struggles.

The other thing we learn from Annagh is that the transition to agriculture did not happen all at once; socially and culturally people retained their links to an older, wilder way of life. Clearing land was hard work: the skeletons show the wear and tear of vigorous lives and the carrying of heavy weights. This hard-won territory had to be defended, and conversely offered an attractive prize for outsiders.

The grave at Annagh dates from around 500 years earlier than the great Neolithic passage tombs such as Newgrange, but it may reflect the continuation of even older cultural practices. In this regard, the careful arrangement of hunter's apparatus (blade and arrowhead) with a selection of animal bones is particularly resonant. The animal bones were brought specially to the cave, and they represent both the old, wild world and the new order of agriculture. There are bones from a bear, a wolf, a wild boar and a deer—creatures of the forest. There are also bones of sheep and cattle—the domestic beasts raised by farmers. Raghnall Ó Floinn of the National Museum, who led the excavation at Annagh, believes that this arrangement is deliberate and indicates a culture that is still in the midst of a long transition. Farming was the dominant way of life, but the call of the wild was still heard. Even as they cleared land and herded cattle, these local heroes may still have thought of themselves as proud hunters.

5

This ceremonial macehead, found in the chamber of the eastern tomb beneath the great passage tomb at Knowth, Co. Meath in the Boyne Valley, is one of the finest works of art to have survived from Neolithic Europe. The unknown artist took a piece of very hard, pale-grey flint, flecked with patches of brown, and carved each of its six surfaces with diamond shapes and swirling spirals. At the front they seem to form a human face, with the shaft hole as a gaping mouth.

The source of the stone is uncertain (perhaps the Orkney islands), but if the macehead were carved in Ireland, the object suggests that someone on the island had attained a very high degree of technical and artistic sophistication. Archaeologist Joseph Fenwick from NUI Galway has suggested that the precision of the carving could have been attained only with a rotary drill, a 'machine very similar to that used to apply the surface decoration to latter-day prestige objects such as Waterford Crystal'. The association of this extraordinary work with one of the great passage tombs tells us something about the society that constructed those enduringly awe-inspiring monuments. It was rich enough to value highly specialised skills and artistic innovation, and it was becoming increasingly hierarchical with an elite capable of controlling large human and physical resources. Knowth and the other great tombs were statements. As archaeologist Alison Sheridan from National Museums Scotland puts it, 'Quite simply, they were designed to be the largest, most elaborate and most "expensive" monuments ever built'. The deposition of a fabulous object like the macehead at Knowth added to the sense that the tombs were 'a means for conspicuous consumption, designed to express and enhance the prestige of rival groups'.

This prestige was asserted in the tombs in three ways: the possession of awe-inspiring objects like this one; the use of astrological knowledge to demonstrate a link with the celestial world; and the passage of the seasons, what Sheridan calls a hotline to the gods (a phallus-shaped stone, also found at Knowth, suggests that fertility rituals were part of this mystique); and the demonstration of international connections. While small tombs like that in Annagh honoured local heroes, the great tombs were self-consciously European. There are strong parallels between Ireland's megalithic tombs and passage graves on the Iberian peninsula and in northwest France. The likelihood is not that the tomb-builders came from these places, but that they were part of a network of Atlantic connections. Already in Ireland a strong sense of the local co-existed with a desire to be seen as part of the wider world.

6

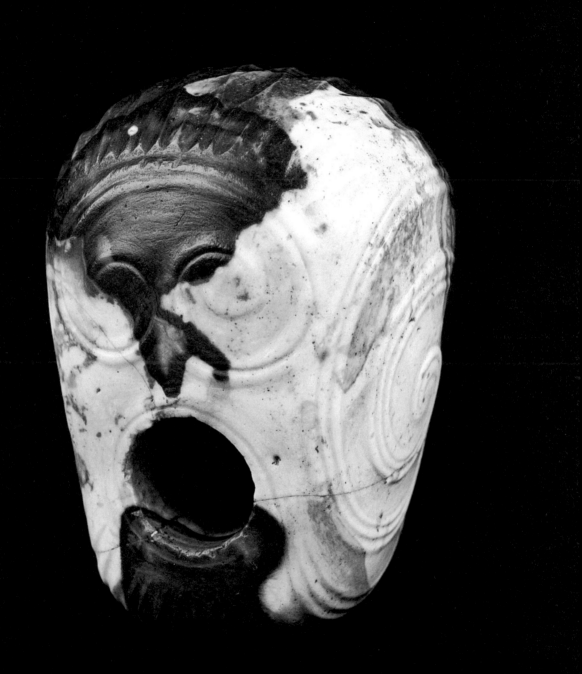

It looks at first like a piece of a rough, greenish mat from a 1970s student flat. In fact it is a 5,000-year-old bag, a very rare survival in Ireland's Neolithic archaeological record of an object of organic material. It was found in a bog in Twyford, Co. Westmeath, and was made by coiling long slivers of wood into spirals that were then bound together with lighter grass-like material. Next, the two sides were woven together along a seam, and handles of plaited straw were added. This would have made for a circular, purse-like bag, about 40cm in diameter, with a narrow opening at the top. It was probably dyed to give it a splash of colour. It offers a glimpse into the everyday life of early Irish farmers. Though we cannot know for sure, there is every chance that it was made and used by a woman.

Similar bags have been found around the world: the technique goes back to the Middle East around 4800 BC and is still used by indigenous cultures. In fact, the best way to get a sense of the Twyford bag is to look at a very similar but intact specimen from nineteenth-century Aboriginal Australia that is also in the National Museum of Ireland. The Twyford bag takes us back into the day-to-day world of Irish people in the fourth millennium BC. Most of what survives from this era is made of hard stone and tends to be associated with ritual, death and power; has the drama of violence and mystery; and is overwhelmingly male. To look at a simple bag that might have been purchased at an ethnic market in a modern city and imagine it in the hands of a Neolithic woman gathering plants or nuts is to be reminded that life, then as now, was dominated by ordinary things and tasks.

What do we know of those ordinary lives? They were short by our standards: most people could not expect to live beyond their 30s. People were probably about the same height as Irish people were in the 1930s: the Neolithic male skeletons found at Annagh in Co. Limerick were about 170cm (5ft 7in) tall. Again from the Annagh skeletons we know they worked hard, but not quite as hard as their counterparts in mediaeval Ireland. They probably wore clothes of leather and woven textiles, such as flax.

We know, too, that they increasingly lived together in relatively substantial settlements of wooden houses, lined with wattle and daub and with thatched roofs. Communities were settling down for the long haul. By the time this bag was made its owner probably lived in a society that had a sense of itself as being old.

9

A man in his late 30s or early 40s was buried alone at Amesbury, near the great English monument of Stonehenge, sometime around 2400–2200 BC.

From the huge range of objects in his grave, he had considerable status. The objects were similar to finds from the same period in Ireland: barbed and tanged arrowheads, a stone wrist guard, beaker-shaped pots. He even wore gold, basket-shaped earrings or hair ornaments. A strikingly similar pair, pictured here, is held in the National Museum in Dublin. In Amesbury, owner and objects were found together, offering far more information than similar isolated artefacts found in Ireland; and, although we must be cautious in our interpretations, information we can glean from Amesbury is likely also true of Ireland. What makes the Amesbury man so significant for an understanding of Irish prehistory is where he came from and the fact that copper knives and other tools in the grave show that he was a metalworker.

By studying the isotopes in his teeth, scientists have established that the 'Amesbury Archer' grew up in the Alpine region of southern Germany or Switzerland, where the mining and use of copper and gold had long been known. Andrew Fitzpatrick, Head of Communications at Wessex Archaeology in Salisbury, suggests, from the evidence of some of the grave goods, that the archer probably made his way to England via southern France, the Iberian peninsula and the Atlantic. Why does he matter for Ireland? The Amesbury Archer provides crucial evidence about the biggest development following the emergence of agriculture: the mining and shaping of metals.

There is no dispute that the advent of metalworking in Ireland, around 2400 BC, is linked to new cultural practices characterised by the kind of objects found in the archer's grave and by the practice of single rather than communal burial. What is not clear, though, is, as Mary Cahill of the National Museum puts it, 'whether it was brought by people on the move looking for new sources of metals or whether it is a transmission of information as opposed to of people. But the fact that the Amesbury Archer turns out not to have been born in southern Britain and has travelled all the way from central Europe is indicative of some movement of people'. We know that by about 2400 BC Ross Island in the Killarney lakes was perhaps the most important copper mine in northwestern Europe. The first Irish evidence of metalworking is therefore already quite highly developed. It is unlikely that this expertise emerged spontaneously. As Fitzpatrick puts it, 'Ross has to be developed by people who already have the knowledge. You cannot just make that up'. A large cultural shift is under way in Ireland, associated with the mining of copper and gold.

This does not mean that Ireland was 'invaded' by new tribes of metalworkers; but migrants from central Europe and the Atlantic coasts of France and Spain almost certainly played a key part in the end of Stone Age Ireland.

WHERE TO SEE THEM: NATIONAL MUSEUM OF IRELAND-ARCHAEOLOGY, KILDARE STREET, DUBLIN 2; 00-353-1-6777444; WWW.MUSEUM.IE

The working of metals may have come late to Ireland, but the island then became one of the most important metal-producing centres in Europe. Ireland had large resources of copper and gold: new sources of wealth and power.

Early smiths made copper axes and traded them to Britain. That this trade worked both ways is evident from the development of bronze objects. The tin that was alloyed with copper to make the bronze probably came from Devon and Cornwall. The working of metal was a cultural as well as an economic activity. Even into the beginning of the modern era the idea of alchemy—the transformation of one substance into another—combined science with magic. In the Early Bronze Age the ability of metalworkers to turn crude rock into objects of dazzling brightness must have imbued them with some sense of the magical. This must have been especially true of gold, not least because it was extremely rare. The people who sifted gold in streams and rivers in the Mourne Mountains had searched hard for something they knew to be especially precious. It was gold, then as now, that had the brightest aura of ritual significance.

There is a natural connection between the brightness of gold and the power of the sun. In Indo-European languages, including that spoken in Bronze Age Ireland, the word for 'god' is derived from a root meaning 'shine'. We know from the older Irish megalithic tombs that rituals of the sun had deep meaning. That some of this was now focused on gold objects is suggested by the creation of decorated discs of sheet-gold. These were probably attached to a backing material and may have been worn to indicate high political status, high religious status or both.

These discs from Tedavnet, in Co. Monaghan, are by far the biggest and most sophisticated yet found; their crosses are elaborated with rows of dots, lines and zig-zag patterns, created using a variety of techniques. The general belief is that they relate to a cult of the sun and that the cruciform shapes in the design are intended to represent its life-giving rays. There is little direct evidence of this cult in Ireland, but rock-art images from contemporary Denmark clearly show people worshipping the sun, which is represented in the same way as on the Irish discs. The sun, in this cult, may have been a goddess rather than a god. One interpretation of the gold discs is that they were placed as symbolic breasts on the chest of a king, creating an image that fused the leader with the life-giving deity. If this is so, the discs belong to an Irish tradition of associating kingship with the sun that continued long after the arrival of Christianity.

WHERE TO SEE THEM: NATIONAL MUSEUM OF IRELAND-ARCHAEOLOGY, KILDARE STREET, DUBLIN 2; 00-353-1-6677444; WWW.MUSEUM.IE

In April 2009 gardaí in Roscommon announced that they had recovered, from a rubbish skip in Dublin, some rather unusual objects: wrapped in a sheet of paper, and weighing just under 80g between them, they had been in a safe stolen from a pharmacy in Strokestown.

Following the robbery, the owners told investigating gardaí that the safe had contained three pieces of gold jewellery. From the description provided, curators from the National Museum believed the jewellery to be gold ornaments of the Early Bronze Age period. Due to the thin and flat nature of the objects and their extremely light weight (78g in total, about 2½ ozs), it became apparent that the thieves might have entirely missed them. What the gardaí recovered from the smelly skip were an Early Bronze Age lunula—a crescent-shaped collar—and two gold discs of the kind found at Tedavnet. The lunula (the word was first applied in the eighteenth century and is Latin for 'little moon') was made by beating gold into a very thin sheet on which decorations were incised or impressed with considerable skill. Like other lunulae, the Coggalbeg example is a very

clever object: producing a highly impressive and seemingly large token of high status from a relatively small amount of gold.

The ornaments, which had been dug up from a bog at Coggalbeg, Co. Roscommon, in 1945, make up a unique assemblage of objects. They represent 'the first time ever that we have an association between the discs and the lunula, because the discs would be considered amongst the earliest gold ornaments and the lunula as coming a little bit later', says Mary Cahill of the National Museum. The appearance of discs and a lunula together opens up the possibility that they may have functioned as part of the same set of regalia, with the discs representing the sun and the lunula the moon. More than 80 of the 100-plus gold lunulae found in western Europe come from Ireland; thus offering the first strong evidence we have of a distinctively Irish cultural form in gold. Instead of Ireland adopting influences from abroad, the process in this case seems to work the other way: Irish gold lunulae spread to Britain, and their shape is copied in necklaces of other materials, such as jet and amber.

14

Sometime in the Early Bronze Age, Irish people began to bury their dead in single graves. This suggests something about their attitude to death and, perhaps more importantly, hints at their attitude to life. A notion is emerging that what is significant is not just the life of the community or of political or religious leaders. Individual lives matter. Not only are the dead given an individual burial, but the idea also takes hold that they will continue in some other form.

'There seems to be a change', says Éamonn Kelly of the National Museum, 'from the more communal approach of the great megalithic tombs to a more individualistic approach. This suggests that there was some sort of a change in how society was organised'.

These pots are among the many 'food vessels' that survive from this period, some of which are vase-shaped, some bowl-shaped. The abstract geometric decoration found on bowls of the era is very similar to that on Irish metalwork of the same period, especially on the gold lunulae. On the base of some pots is a starburst pattern that may relate to a sun cult.

The vessels were made to be buried with the dead. The graves are generally just large enough to hold the body and the accompanying pots. Adding to this sense of a new awareness of the individual is an apparently wide choice of burial forms. Some members of the community do not seem to have been accorded a formal burial at all. Those who were, experienced an extraordinary and shifting diversity of funerary rituals: cremation, unburnt burial, disarticulated remains, multiple burials, pit graves, cist graves, flat graves and graves in or under mounds all occur over the five or six centuries before 1500 BC. Thereafter burials are rare in the Bronze Age.

To our eyes, the most moving of these burials are those in which the dead person has been arranged in a foetal position. Why were the dead placed as if they were curled up in the womb? The obvious suggestion is of a simple and beautiful metaphor: the tomb is a womb. The dead are to be reborn into another life. The drink or food in the vessel is meant to sustain them on the journey from one state to the other. This tells us both that these Bronze Age people were looking carefully at the human body: they knew the shape of the child in the womb; and that this capacity to observe humanity went hand in hand with a desire to transcend it.

WHERE TO SEE THEM: NATIONAL MUSEUM OF IRELAND-ARCHAEOLOGY, KILDARE STREET, DUBLIN 2; 00-353-1-6777444; WWW.MUSEUM.IE

In 1810, a boy digging close to the ringed fort known as the Rath of the Synods on the Hill of Tara in Co. Meath found two magnificent gold torcs. They had been made with considerable skill by hammering the edges of a gold bar into four thin flanges on an anvil and then twisting the whole lot into a circle. The amount of gold used to make them, the fact that torcs are a new kind of object, the technological sophistication they required and the emergence of Tara itself as an especially important ritual centre all point to a society that is becoming more complex.

The largest of the torcs has a diameter of about 42cm and, if untwisted, would extend to about 167cm. The ability to make objects such as these comes in a period of development that may have been stimulated by the deterioration of the Irish climate from about 1200 BC. This may have led to conflict and insecurity (new types of weapons and enclosed settlements date from this period), with the emergence of more powerful kings. The assumption is that torcs were worn around the neck, but these from Tara are large enough to have to been worn around the waist; they could even have been placed on idols. The strong likelihood, however, is that they were, as Eamonn Kelly of the National Museum puts it, 'regalia worn by the kings of Tara. How do we know? These are the finest objects of the period'.

At the beginning of the Late Bronze Age, complex twisting techniques replaced sheet goldwork. Whereas the older lunulae were a very clever way of making the most of a small amount of precious gold, the torcs seem to be designed to show off the amount of gold used to create them. They are intended for ostentatious display. Tara had been an important centre for three millennia before the torcs were made, but their awesome quality suggests that it had become considerably more so. 'You get the sense', says Kelly, 'that Tara was not just about political power or even religious power. It is a spiritual power. This is what gives the kings their authority. There is already a sense of that in these objects. They identify the one wearing them as the person who connects this world to the other world'.

WHERE TO SEE THEM: NATIONAL MUSEUM OF IRELAND-ARCHAEOLOGY, KILDARE STREET, DUBLIN 2; 00-353-1-6777444; WWW.MUSEUM.IE

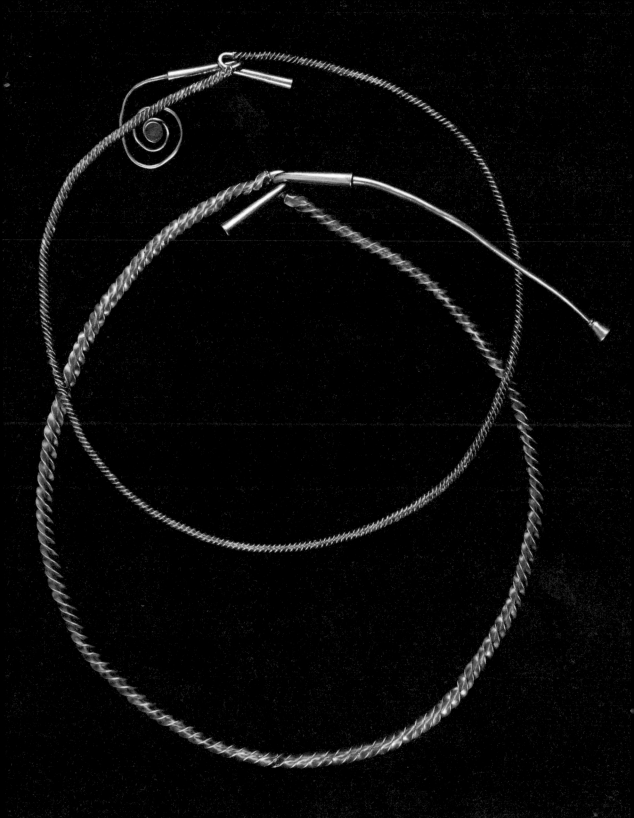

A little under 3,000 years ago someone in Ireland was very, very rich. In March 1854 a ganger ordered some navvies working on the construction of the West Clare Railway near Newmarket-on-Fergus to straighten a dyke running close to the small lake of Mooghaun. They shifted a stone and found a small, rough chamber with a flagstone on top. When they opened it they uncovered one of the largest hoards of Bronze Age gold objects ever found in western or northern Europe. The navvies filled their pockets and 'disposed each of his share to travelling dealers'. Many pieces were melted down, but the evidence suggests there were 138 bracelets, six collars, possibly two torcs and four other pieces: 150 objects, all of gold. The 29 objects that survive, split between the National Museum of Ireland in Dublin and the British Museum in London, are not especially remarkable in themselves. Most of the hoard consists of relatively simple bracelets, whose more or less uniform design has prompted suggestions that they may have been merely a way of storing the gold. What is extraordinary is the sheer scale of the wealth they represent.

Mooghaun has a large and prominent hill-fort, with three huge, roughly concentric stone ramparts enclosing about 12 hectares and commanding wide views of the Shannon estuary. The fort may have been a ritual centre serving as the capital of the wider region. Pollen analysis from Mooghaun lake shows that the area was intensively farmed at the time. The wealth of the hoard suggests, however, that the Shannon estuary was also being used for fishing and trading. There must have been a long period of stability and prosperity in which such riches could be accumulated.

There are other huge hoards from this period, notably one of 200 bronze objects from Dowris, near Birr, in Co. Offaly. That great find gave its name to the major phase of the Late Bronze Age in Ireland. The Dowris hoard was found in or near a body of water called Lough Coura. The lake no longer exists, but in the early-nineteenth century it formed an area of open water. In late prehistoric times it was probably much more extensive. The term hoard was applied to the Dowris find because it was assumed that it represented a collection of objects all deposited at the same time, but the range of material and its watery context suggest that it may have been a diverse set of objects (bronze swords, spears, cauldrons, horns) deposited perhaps over several centuries.

Were the Dowris, Mooghaun and other hoards buried as votive offerings to the gods, or merely for safe keeping? The Mooghaun hoard's siting near a lake might point to the former, but the stone chamber in which it was buried suggests that the gold was meant to be accessible to its owners. Hoards such as these tell a story of human motives that were probably a blend of protection of material wealth, preservation of memory and propitiation of supernatural powers. Either way, the Mooghaun hoard tells us of an Ireland characterised, in the words of archaeologists Andrew Halpin and Conor Newman, as 'one of old wealth, stability and cultural homogeneity'. In a literal sense, at least, this was a golden age Like all such ages, it was not to last.

21

 WHERE TO SEE IT: NATIONAL MUSEUM OF IRELAND-ARCHAEOLOGY, KILDARE STREET, DUBLIN 2; 00-353-1-6777444; WWW.MUSEUM.IE, AND BRITISH MUSEUM, GREAT RUSSELL STREET, LONDON WC1B 3DG; 00-44-20-7323-8299; WWW.BRITISHMUSEUM.ORG

The marks that run through the ridges on the right-hand side of this dazzling gold collar show that it was roughly bent in two before being thrust into a rock fissure in the Burren, in Co. Clare, where it was found by a boy hunting rabbits in 1932. This folding is no accident: most of the other eight surviving examples of this uniquely Irish object were bent in the same way. They were, it seems, 'decommissioned' before being buried; such was their power that they had to be broken before being let out of the hands of their owners.

The Gleninsheen gorget is a technical and artistic achievement at the apex of goldworking in the Europe of its time. It was made by applying a range of techniques: repoussé, chasing, raising, stamping, twisting and stitching. The discs at the terminals of the collar are decorated with spiral patterns of extraordinary finesse. This kind of work, examples of which are heavily concentrated in Munster, can only have come from a highly evolved society with a population dense enough to support specialist artists, and sufficiently settled to develop its own sophisticated traditions.

There is evidence that gorgets like this one may be an ultra-luxurious and superfine expression of a contemporary European fashion. On mainland Europe c. 1200 BC one of the most important high-status objects is the bronze cuirass, a piece of armour that fits the whole torso. This highly decorated armour is evidence of the emer-gence of a prestigious warrior caste. Bronze cuirasses are not found in Ireland (Irish warriors probably favoured leather body armour and leather helmets), but Mary Cahill of the National Museum has pointed out detailed similarities in structure and decoration between Irish gorgets and European cuirasses: the raised lines on the Gleninsheen collar match the lines on the armour that indicate the warrior's ribs; the circular discs mimic the breast and nipples. What we have, then, is a very specific Irish version of the symbols of a European warrior cult. In Europe the object is bronze and takes the literal shape of the war-rior's body; in Ireland it is gold and abstract. Who needs ordinary bronze when the overwhelming symbolic power of gold can be harnessed?

The gorget may be a more self-consciously artistic representation of a European style, but it nonetheless belongs to the common ideal of a warrior elite. A rare rock carving from southwest-ern Spain in this period shows a warrior with sword, shield, spear and chariot. The shield has a highly distinctive V-shaped notch. Distinctive, that is, except for the fact that the only extant shield of this kind was found at Cloonbrin, near Abbeyshrule, in Co. Longford. The gorget, there-fore, is a peculiarly Irish and especially refined expression of a warrior cult that extended far beyond Ireland.

100 WHERE TO SEE IT: NATIONAL MUSEUM OF IRELAND-ARCHAEOLOGY, KILDARE STREET, DUBLIN 2; 00-353-1-6777444; WWW.MUSEUM.IE

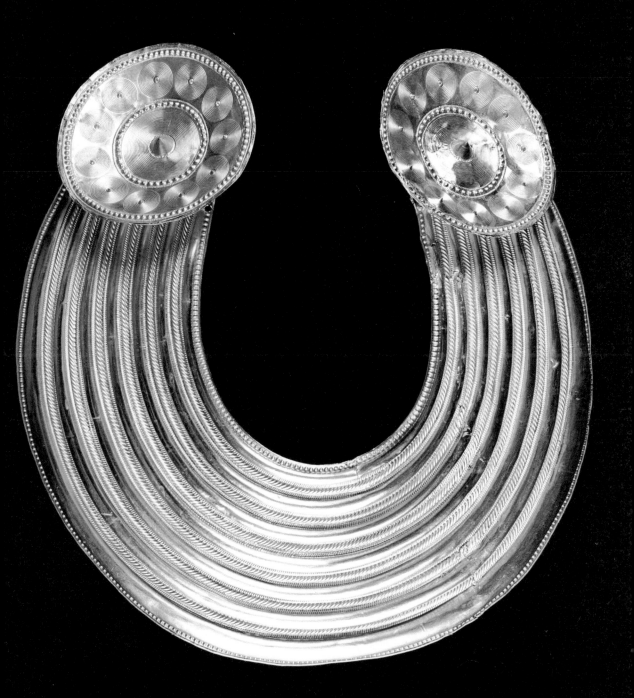

13. CASTLEDERG BRONZE CAULDRON, 700–600BC

Christianity may not have been the first Mediterranean religion to find its way to Ireland.

The most famous Irish legend, the Táin Bó Cualinge, centres on the struggle for control of a magical bull. It thus suggests distant echoes of the presence in Bronze Age Ireland of a bull cult that itself originated millennia before in the eastern Aegean Sea. Versions of this cult spread into the Iberian peninsula, and it would not be surprising if it resonated with Ireland's cattle-rearing society.

This magnificent bronze cauldron, found in a bog in Castlederg, Co. Tyrone, is crafted from offset bands of sheet bronze held in place by rows of conical rivets. It could be seen simply as an expression of a chieftain's bounty in feasting his followers, but it almost certainly had a ritual as well as a social significance. The skills of casting, beating and riveting required to make it, and the care with which similar cauldrons were repaired from time to time, suggest it was a valuable object and one of very special status. It was probably used as a central part of elite ceremonies in which the local king's ability to share food and drink was an enactment of his power. Cauldrons like this one are at the root of the folk tales of 'cauldrons of plenty' that survived for millennia in Europe.

But that plenty depended on the reign of the 'proper' king. Eamonn Kelly of the National Museum speculates that the cauldron may have been associated with a ritual for the choice of a new king, in which a bull was sacrificed. In his view, the cauldron is best understood in association with two other kinds of objects from the same period that also feature in the huge hoard found at Dowris, Co. Offaly: bronze horns that, when blown, produce 'a deep bass note, resembling the bellowing of a bull'; and so-called crotals, pear-shaped bronze objects that look like hand grenades but were perhaps meant to represent the bull's scrotum. We cannot know for sure whether the cauldron was indeed part of a coherent bull cult, but it is reasonable to see such cauldrons as aristocratic possessions that were put to periodic use. Moreover, the fact that so many have been recovered as single deposits in bogs may indicate a special ceremonial significance.

What is clear is that the practice of using bronze feasting equipment belongs to a widespread central and western European Bronze Age elite fashion. The distribution of such prestigious items as cauldrons, and of swords, shields, personal ornaments and a range of other metal artefacts, shows strong interaction between the aristocratic elements of various European communities, and how elite fashions travelled among them. These are only the most visible expression of inter-relationships that must also have included the movement of less durable items. This Later Bronze Age ferment of activity and the frequent contacts it implies may well be one of the elements in the evolution of a common 'Celtic' language. And for all of these elites, the cauldron expressed the double nature of kingship. It unites ritual power with the most basic fact of life: the need to eat. A ruler who cannot guarantee the one has no right to claim the other.

25

100 WHERE TO SEE IT: NATIONAL MUSEUM OF IRELAND-ARCHAEOLOGY, KILDARE STREET, DUBLIN 2; 00-353-1-6777444; WWW.MUSEUM.IE

The past is unpredictable. This iron spearhead, found in the River Inny at Lackan in Co. Westmeath, is of a kind familiar enough from the Ireland of AD 500. Andy Halpin of the National Museum says that it 'would not be out of place in the early-mediaeval period…When you think of the Iron Age legends of Cúchulainn, this is the type of weapon that people think of them carrying'. The problem is that recent radiocarbon dating of the remains of its wooden shaft suggests that this spear may be more than 1,200 years older than that. If this is so, it explodes a myth about how the Iron Age came to Ireland.

The long-held belief was that the use of iron in Ireland was a result of the invasion of the Celts. Greek writers refer to the existence of 'Keltoi' in central Europe in the sixth century BC. It seemed logical that the 'sudden' appearance of iron in Ireland must be evidence of the arrival of these Celts. Conversely, if there was no late and sudden arrival of iron, the idea of a Celtic invasion looks highly dubious.

No one doubts that the influence of these central Europeans is evident in some Irish artefacts from the third century BC onwards. There are, however, no Irish metal artefacts, never mind ones with continental influence, between 600 and 300 BC. Iron corrodes and is very hard to date.

So far, Iron Age iron objects found in Ireland have been pretty crude and relatively late, dating no earlier than 300 BC. The Lackan spearhead, though, is certainly not crude: it is elegantly made. It is almost freakishly well-preserved: it would be unusual to find a weapon from the Middle Ages in such good condition. It is not an obvious import. And it seems to be very, very old. The radiocarbon tests date the ash shaft somewhere between 811 and 673 BC. Halpin urges caution, but there is no reason why this date has to be regarded as wrong.

It is the combination of this early date and its superb quality that makes this spear so startling. 'We are beginning', says Halpin, 'to get other evidence for ironworking technology at an earlier date than we thought. The idea that ironworking was happening here in maybe 600 or 700 BC would not really be disputed any more. But the idea that something as fine as this was being produced at that period suggests not only that iron was being worked here, but also that it was being worked by very competent smiths much earlier than we think'.

Those smiths were not invading 'Celts'. They may well have been part of the same culture that was producing the dazzling gold and bronze objects we have already seen.

WHERE TO SEE IT: NATIONAL MUSEUM OF IRELAND-ARCHAEOLOGY, KILDARE STREET, DUBLIN 2; 00-353-1-6777444; WWW.MUSEUM.IE

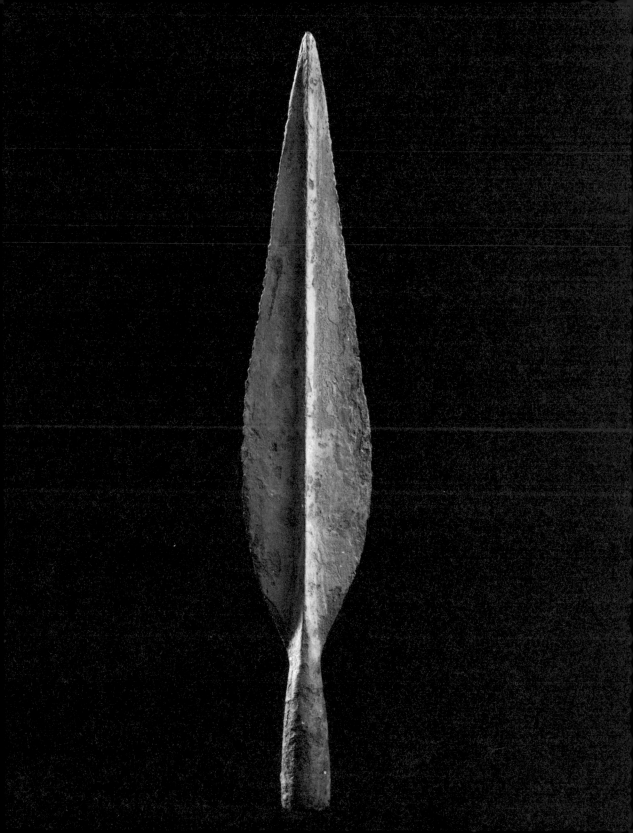

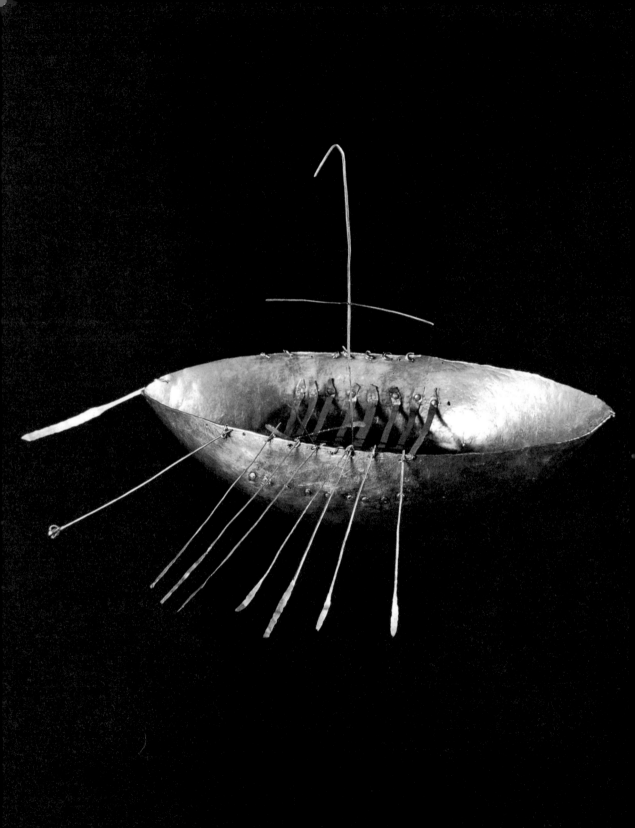

This delightful gold model-boat, just under 20cm long but rich in detail, is a rare thing in early Irish art: a realistic depiction of a real object. It appears to be a precise model of an ocean-going vessel, probably wooden but possibly made of hide. The boat originally had nine benches for the rowers and eighteen oars with rowlocks, a long oar for steering at the stern, three forked barge-poles, a grappling-iron or anchor and a mast. This might have been the kind of boat in which Irish people traded with Britain and western Europe, bringing back not only goods but also ideas, technologies and fashions.

The realism of the boat does not mean, however, that it was not also symbolic. It was contained in a hoard of gold objects found in what had once been a salt-marsh on the shore at Lough Foyle, in Broighter, Co. Derry. The hoard might have been a votive offering to the sea god Manannán Mac Lir. The sea was, as it still is today, an unpredictable force. Manannán, who ruled his otherworld kingdom and could ride out over the waves on his chariot, was the ultimate master mariner, impervious to the sea's deadly turbulence. It is easy to understand why those who sailed in open boats like this one would seek his help and protection. Apart from the delight of the boat itself, what is striking is that the gold objects found with it are mostly imports, including two neck chains that come from the eastern Mediterranean, possibly from Roman Egypt.

Ireland, which had previously been the great producer of goldwork in western Europe, is now bringing it in from the outside. What has happened to the people who once had such staggering wealth in bronze and gold? Have they been displaced by those who use the new metal, iron? One possibility is that the change from bronze and gold to iron is evidence of a shift in social power. Those lower down the social scale start to use the cheaper iron, challenging the dominance of the elites who controlled the bronze industry. It is striking that many of the early iron objects in Ireland are practical working tools, especially axes. As archaeologist John Waddell puts it, 'it is possible that the hewers of wood rather than the yielders of swords were the beneficiaries of the new iron technology'. This may be one of the reasons why the burial of gold and bronze objects as offerings to the gods declines after 700 BC.

Whatever shifts of power were taking place within Ireland, the beauty of the Broighter boat and the care lavished on its creation suggest that trade with the world beyond its shores was one of the drivers of change.

29

The dazzling regalia that survives from ancient Ireland suggests that the rulers of the time had enormous prestige, both physical and spiritual. By the Early Iron Age at least, however, power had become highly conditional. The deal for the ruler was clear and brutal: produce the goods or be ritually slaughtered and sacrificed. If the king could not guarantee peace and prosperity, he was sent back into the land to which he was ritually wed.

In 2003, shortly after a well-preserved Iron Age body was found in a bog in Clonycavan, Co. Meath, another was found at Croghan Hill in Old Croghan, Co. Offaly. Both bodies, on close examination, had the marks of high status. Clonycavan Man's hair contains an imported gel. Old-croghan Man has a leather and tinned bronze armlet, with stamped metal clips representing the sun and decorated in the fashionable continental style, on his arm. His hands show no sign of manual labour, implying special or aristocratic status.

Most bog bodies are a tribute to the preservative qualities of Irish bogs and provide important information on dress, etc. Such bodies are often clothed and represent accidental death or casual burial; most are of mediaeval or more recent date. A very small number of bog bodies are Iron Age sacrifices of naked or nearly naked males, providing grim proof of sinister rituals. These bog bodies appear to have been 'killed' three times: by strangulation, by stabbing and by drowning. However ritualised, Old-croghan Man's death was garishly violent. Hazel rods that may be the remains of a spansel were threaded through holes in his upper arms. He was stabbed in the chest, struck in the neck, decapitated and cut in half. (All that has been found is his torso and arms.) But the violence was not mere sadism. 'This', says Eamonn Kelly of the National Museum, 'is not done for torture or to inflict pain. It is a triple killing because the goddess to whom the sacrifice is made has three natures. She is goddess of sovereignty, of fertility and of war/death. So sacrifices are made to her in all her forms'.

Poignantly, Old-croghan Man has a wound on his arm, which he lifted instinctively to try to shield himself from the weapon with which he was stabbed in the chest. Before his death, he was fed a ritual meal of milk and grain: not the high-status meat-based diet that is revealed by analysis of his nails, but one meant, rather, to symbolise the earth's fertility. He had been a huge man, almost six-feet-three-inches tall. It is easy to imagine him as a champion or hero. He was young and healthy, and, as mentioned, there is little sign that he did physical labour. The bog where his body is found is close to the foot of the hill where the kings of the Uí Failge were inaugurated.

This culture of brutal sacrifice may tell us something about the mood of the times. In the last centuries BC, Ireland became colder and wetter. Food may have been more scarce. The great prestige of those who ruled had always been linked to their claim to reflect the views of the other world. When times were bad, this very claim became fatal.

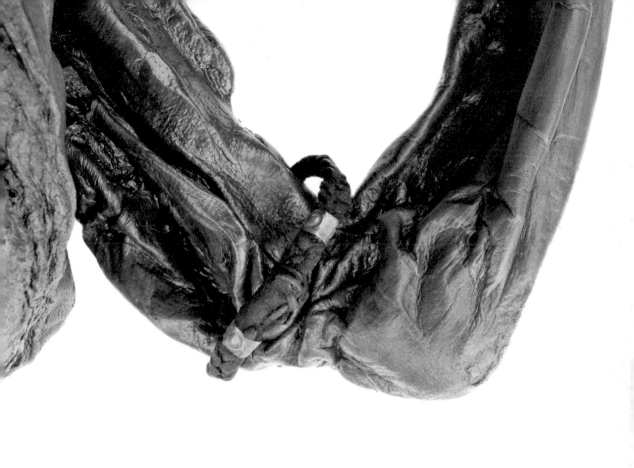

One of the most famous pieces of ancient sculpture is The Dying Gaul, until recently regarded as a Roman copy of a lost Greek original of *c*. 220 BC from Pergamon in Asia Minor. It may in fact be an original. It is an arresting and deeply moving image of a naked warrior lying on his shield, a gaping wound in his side, his head bowed, awaiting death. The original was almost certainly commissioned to commemorate a Greek victory over the Celtic Galatians, and as such it provides easily the most memorable visual image of the Celts. The Dying Gaul is sometimes called 'The Dying Trumpeter': coiled around the warrior's legs is a large, curved, bronze trumpet. Trumpets such as this were used in battle by Celtic peoples. The Roman historian Polybius wrote of one battle that 'the noise of the Celtic host terrified the Romans; for there were countless trumpeters and horn blowers and…the whole army was shouting its war cries at the same time'.

This splendid bronze trumpet, one of four found in a dried-up lake at Loughnashade ('lake of the treasures'), near the important royal centre of Emain Macha, in Co. Armagh, is similar to the one at the feet of The Dying Gaul and to those that so terrified the Romans. It is an outstanding piece of Celtic art. The main section of the tube is a masterpiece of skilled riveting. The bell end is superbly decorated with a lotus-bud motif, the origins of which lie in Mediterranean art. The style, with elaborate curved patterns, is that of high Celtic art, called La Tène after a site in Switzerland, and it would dominate Irish art for many centuries.

The Loughnashade trumpet is thus strong evidence of Celtic influence in Ireland. Does it mark what is still referred to as 'the coming of the Celts'? No. La Tène objects of this period are rare and heavily associated with a warrior aristocracy. There is simply no evidence of a large-scale invasion of Ireland by new peoples. What about the Irish language, which is part of the Celtic linguistic family? There is no reason to suppose that it arrived in Ireland with invaders during the Iron Age. It is probably much older. Barry Cunliffe suggests that contacts between what he calls the communities of the 'Atlantic zone' were intensified in the period 1300–800 BC. 'It would not be surprising to find the development of broadly similar languages evolving out of the common Indo-European' with which they all started. What the Loughnashade trumpet tells us, therefore, is that there were strong contacts between Ireland and the European continent in the last century BC, as had been the case for thousands of years, and that over the course of that time some Irish elites adopted influences from the latest European style.

33

There was no Celtic invasion of Ireland. This does not mean, however, that the island was un-affected by the upheavals in Celtic Europe caused by another invasion: the spread of the Roman Empire into Gaul and Britain.

In the decades after 60 BC, Rome pushed its frontiers northwards through Gaul (roughly today's France) to the Rhine, and westwards to the Atlantic. In 43 BC, Emperor Claudius set in train the full-scale invasion that gradually created the Roman province of Britannia. The conquest of Britain was slow and violent, and the shock waves were certainly felt in Ireland. This small bronze bowl, found in a tributary of the Shannon in Co. Leitrim, was polished to a fine finish on a lathe. Its glory, however, is the superb handle, cast in the shape of a bird's head with a long, curving neck, an upturned beak and big, staring eyes that were once inlaid with glass or enamel. It is prob-ably a stylised version of a duck. Birds have a strongly supernatural aspect in early Irish culture, as messengers from the otherworld or mediators between gods and humans. The bowl was thus probably used in drinking bouts that had a ritual as well as a social function: we know that a drink-ing ceremony was part of royal inaugurations.

The Keshcarrigan bowl is similar to examples in bronze found in Devon and Cornwall and in Brittany. In a further reflection of Atlantic links, Armorican potters probably copied similar vessels in pottery; there is a horse-head bowl from Hennebont on the Côtes d'Armor, for instance.

The Keshcarrigan bowl may have been made in Ireland (a hoard with similar objects has been found near Ballinasloe, Co. Galway) but using British prototypes. There is little doubt that it rep-resents some movement of people into Ireland. Some of the Gallic Belgic tribes crossed into Britain as refugees from the Romans, displacing native people. These movements of population reached Ireland in the century before and the one following the birth of Christ.

Southwestern England had connections with Ireland going back thousands of years: Cornish tin was used to make Irish bronze. It is not surprising that, in times of stress, trading contacts would deepen into actual movement of people. A bowl similar to this one, found at Fore, Co. Westmeath, is associated with what seems to be a Gallo-British-type burial and perhaps also with a Roman boat. The technique of finishing the Keshcarrigan bowl with a lathe is also new to Ireland, though it becomes central to later Irish art, including that of the Ardagh and Derrynaflan chalices.

There is a cemetery on Lambay Island, Co. Dublin, dating perhaps a little later than the Keshcarrigan bowl, that contains the remains of people from north Britain, possibly well-to-do members of the Brigantes, a tribe whose revolt against the Romans was crushed in AD 74. Roman expansion was the central fact of European life at this time. Ireland could not es-cape its consequences.

IOO WHERE TO SEE IT: NATIONAL MUSEUM OF IRELAND-ARCHAEOLOGY, KILDARE STREET, DUBLIN 2; 00-353-1-6777444; WWW.MUSEUM.IE

Until the late-nineteenth century, Corleck Hill, in the Co. Cavan townland of Drumeague, was the site of a Lughnasa festival held on the first Sunday of August. Lughnasa was one of the great quarterly feasts of the old Irish year, and it also retained millennia-old memories of the Celtic god Lugh. The Lughnasa festival, which continues to be celebrated in Ireland to this day, ran over three days, echoing the idea of a tripartite deity. (It is now celebrated on the Sunday closest to 1 August, with the most celebrated event being the annual pilgrimage to the top of Croagh Patrick in Co. Mayo).

This potently enigmatic stone head was found c. 1855 near Corleck Hill. Carved into a 32cm-high piece of rounded sandstone are three broadly similar faces, all with narrow mouths, bossed eyes and remote, implacable expressions. A small hole in the base of the head suggests that it was secured to some kind of pedestal. One of the mouths also has a small circular hole, a feature that links it to several carved heads from Yorkshire. This link to Roman Britain reminds us that Ireland is, at this time, on the cusp of the Roman world. Even if the Corleck Head represents a new variant in religious practice, however, it also speaks to us of an astonishing continuity.

The head is often taken to represent an 'all-knowing god', who can see all dimensions of reality, but its three faces also link us back to much older traditions of the three-natured goddess. The 'power of three' is an important theme of Celtic art and is represented in the common symbol of the triskel, or triskelion: three interlocked spirals. It relates to the triple nature of the great goddess, the Morrígan: sovereignty, fertility and death; it is also common in Romano-British art, through the figures of the Matronae, the three ancestral mothers, representing strength, power and fertility. The Corleck Head, which is neither obviously male nor female, and which can be seen to unite old Irish and new Romano-British cults, touches all of these nerves.

In the context of the Lughnasa festival, the head may represent the old god Crum Dubh, who was buried for three days with only his head above ground, so that the young Lugh could temporarily take his place. Máire MacNeill, in her classic *The festival of Lughnasa*, suggests that

> there was a custom of bringing a stone head from a nearby sanctuary and placing it on the top of the hill for the duration of the festival. The head looking in different directions may be… looking propitiously on the ripening corn-plots.

That something of this ritual survived in modern Ireland (and into Brian Friel's play 'Dancing at Lughnasa') is spine-tingling but not entirely illogical. The Corleck Head may represent a late expression of pre-Christian religion, but it also points forward to a religion that was beginning to spread from the Mediterranean—the one with three persons in one God.

100 WHERE TO SEE IT: NATIONAL MUSEUM OF IRELAND-ARCHAEOLOGY, KILDARE STREET, DUBLIN 2; 00-353-1-6777444; WWW.MUSEUM.IE

The Vikings did not wear horned helmets. The Iron Age Irish did wear head-dresses with what look like horns on them. There are two outstanding examples, the 'Cork horns' (at Cork Public Museum) and the Petrie 'crown', so called because it came from the collection of the nineteenth-century antiquarian, George Petrie. Petrie either did not know or did not record where the object was originally found.

The 'crown' consists of a sheet of bronze with a pair of highly decorated discs attached to its front. The design on the discs is a highly stylised representation of a solar boat: the sun being carried across the heavens in a boat with a bird's head prow and stern. Its presence on the Petrie 'crown' offers a rare insight into prehistoric religious beliefs, reflecting a complex solar cosmology that Ireland's early inhabitants apparently shared with their European neighbours. Each disc supported a conical horn, only one of which survives. This complex bronze arrangement was then sewn on to a leather or textile band to form a head-dress. The very high quality of the decoration and riveting suggests that this was worn by a particularly powerful figure.

This power may have derived from links to Roman Britain. The horned head-dresses are a new phenomenon, utilising new casting technologies and showing off the high-end design of the European Iron Age culture known as La Tène. The Roman general Agricola remarked that Ireland could be taken with 'one legion and a moderate number of auxiliaries'. It is possible that some kind of invasion was attempted. The Roman poet Juvenal records that 'we have taken our arms beyond the shores of Ireland'. If this did happen, the invasion was either beaten back or the Romans decided that Ireland was not worth the effort of conquest.

They did, however, trade with Ireland. The historian Tacitus notes of the island in the first century that 'the interior parts are little known, but through commercial intercourse and the merchants, there is better knowledge of the harbours and approaches'. The Irish imported goods from the Roman world, as we have seen from the presence of the Egyptian necklace in the Broighter hoard. There are Roman objects from the royal site at Tara, and there is even the skull of a Barbary ape from Navan Fort, in Co. Armagh. The trade went both ways, however; Roman Britain, with its cities and standing army, offered a thriving marketplace.

'The development of urban centres', says Eamonn Kelly of the National Museum of Ireland, 'means there was demand for cattle on the hoof. The Roman army consumed large amounts of leather. They were importing hide, and they were probably importing butter as well. Those who can exploit these trade connections come from the rich grazing lands, and they will go on to form the core of Ireland's mediaeval dynasties'.

100 WHERE TO SEE IT: NATIONAL MUSEUM OF IRELAND-ARCHAEOLOGY, KILDARE STREET, DUBLIN 2; 00-353-1-6777444; WWW.MUSEUM.IE

It is a broken gravestone, with a crude inscription: CVNORIX MACVSMA [Q]VICO[L]I[N]E. The slab, found in 1967, had probably been re-used from someone else's burial. Yet it is resonant of the way Irish invaders and raiders took advantage of the collapse of Roman Britain.

The slab was found in Wroxeter, near Shrewsbury in the western English county of Shropshire. This village was once Viroconium, the fourth-largest city in Roman Britain, a thriving hub of 5,000 people—about the same size as Pompeii. After the Roman legions were withdrawn from Britain, in 410, even places as far inland as Viroconium became vulnerable to attack from Irish raiders. The significance of this gravestone is that the inscription is in a partly Latinised version of the Irish language. It means 'Hound-king, son of the tribe of Holly'. Cunorix was Irish, and the existence of the stone suggests that he had become a powerful figure in this part of England.

From the fourth century AD the Romans were building forts on the west coast of Britain (at Holyhead and Cardiff) to defend against the Irish raiders they called 'Scotti' (the name survives as Scotland). We know from the Roman writer Ammianus that diplomatic relations had been established with the Scotti but that in AD 360 the breaking of a treaty led to devastating raids from both Ireland and Scotland. The ability to mount major seaborne raids suggests a resurgence of wealth in Ireland, connected to the expansion of agriculture and the building of huge numbers of stone ring-forts. As Roman power collapsed entirely, Irish raiders were followed to Britain by Irish settlers. The most important colony was at Dyfed in southwest Wales, but Argyll in western Scotland, the Isle of Man and parts of southwest England were also colonised.

This expansionary drive had huge consequences in Ireland. The Romans had done deals with, and helped to keep in place, the old kingships in Ireland. The new money that both funded and resulted from attacks on Britain, however, allowed the formation of numerous small tribal units, or *túatha*. 'There were', says Conor Newman of NUI Galway, 'new kids on the block in these centuries. Before the fourth or fifth centuries you have five great royal sites. It is not coincidental that Roman material has turned up at all of those sites. Afterwards, the country is fragmented into 150 smaller *túatha*. Something pretty radical has happened. I think it is the impact of the collapse of the Roman Empire on Ireland. Britain becomes an open cash register for Irish raiders. Things are being robbed—and so are people. The status quo is undermined'.

For the existing British population, much of this was deeply unpleasant, but the colonisations did result in much closer ties between the two islands and a stronger British influence on Irish culture. Ironically, one long-term result was the spread from Britain to Ireland of what had become the official Roman religion.

41

22. ST. PATRICK'S *CONFESSIO*, C.AD460-90

Ego Patricius, peccator rusticissimus et minimus omnium fidelium et contemptibilis sum apud plurimos… 'My name is Patrick. I am a sinner, a simple country person, and the least of all believers. I am looked down upon by many…'

These artfully humble words mark three immense moments in the development of Irish culture. First, along with Patrick's Letter to Coroticus, it is the oldest surviving piece of prose writing done in Ireland, and so signals one immense change: the arrival of literacy. Second, Patrick is the first person in Ireland who can, through these texts, be positively identified as an individual with a known life story. This, in other words, is the moment when prehistory ends and Irish history begins. Third, of course, Patrick's 'Confession' speaks to us of one of the most paradoxical but profound developments in that Irish history. On the one hand, it is a dramatic narrative of the collapse of the Roman Empire. As he relates it, Patrick, son of a noble Romano-British family, is kidnapped at the age of sixteen and enslaved as a herdsman by Irish raiders who no longer fear the might of Rome. On the other, just as Roman power is vanishing, Patrick brings it to Ireland in another form: Christianity.

Patrick was not the first Christian missionary to Ireland. Palladius, probably from Auxerre, in France, was sent in 431 as the first bishop to 'the Irish believing in Christ'—a pre-existing Irish Christian community. Some of these early Irish Christians may have been, like Patrick himself, slaves captured in Britain.

Patrick, however, as he says in the *Confessio*, preached the Gospel 'unto those parts beyond which there lives nobody'. Tradition places the hub of his mission in Armagh. Patrick claims that

> in Ireland, where they never had any knowledge of God but, always, until now, cherished idols and unclean things, they are lately become a people of the Lord, and are called children of God; the sons of the Irish and the daughters of the chieftains are to be seen as monks and virgins of Christ.

This overstates the speed of the movement from the old religion to the new, but it reflects the reality that Patrick played a key role in the spread of Irish Christianity.

Pictured is the earliest surviving manuscript copy, made around 807 by the scribe Ferdomnach in Armagh. (Its opening words appear on folio 22r of the *Book of Armagh*, which is displayed with the *Book of Kells* at Trinity College Dublin.) It leaves out those parts of the 'confession' in which Patrick mentions his own failures and weaknesses: for the later monks who were involved in establishing his cult, it was important to show him as a powerful worker of wonders. Most probably, while he was alive, it was his humility and simplicity that made Patrick so attractive and persuasive.

WHERE TO SEE IT: OLD LIBRARY, TRINITY COLLEGE DUBLIN; 00-353-1-8962320; WWW.TCD.IE/LIBRARY/BOOKOFKELLS; SEE ALSO WWW.CONFESSIO.IE/MANUSCRIPTS

habent unum xpe pr illum illam q:
mntuch multar pretier
Uir e rex xpianer uincim ait
O mea beata parruchia tua s
puincia tua qs reputabitur m
nanchiam quam inparte troysci
tali 7 occidentali domintu s ineuisse

IИCIPIТ LIBЯ ЯEX PЯIMUS INCIPIT

ETI PЯIMCIT pЯELATORUM
cirssimur de mimmu sem
nium Ыdelim de CONTEMPTIBILIT
Ыem qs plurimor

PОЯЯEX Ыbui Calponnium dia
conum Ыlium eЫidam poЯti
Ыerbei qui Ыint unio bannaudin
Zabchinue uillulam cum ppe Ыbs
ubi eo chpterram decit Armonium
inam zune Ыuit xii Dmiuum 1s
nonabam de hiberione incap Ыnita
de Alducer pum cum emilia
hominum Яe Ыlummouiza nЫu
q Ыtlo noch Ыmur 7 pseptrar 1s Ыor
Ыhium q Яacendo Ыib mЫ
Ы oboedientii Ыmur qui nЫm Ыa
lctin Ыmonebane de dir mdyx
it Ыupr nor Ыram Ammadomr Яue
de dir ppe nylie Ыtib muler eЫ
Ыy eUultimum chinue ubi nЫ
paruntar mea euodeum int alt
nЫuar de tibi dir Apmut y Ыrz

In Chailunitatii mete ut rmonem ona
pum diucta mea ut confirmanem toto con
de addom dmm Ыu ner pЫr Ыmbuartm
mm 7 mbr Ыur adolupechie 1cnonan
Ыemete 6o Cusfodintme aЫ quam pЫ
pem cum 7 aЫ quam papem e dirpnclhem
e bonum 7 ylum 6o mumimem 6o Con
pulaZur ms ut paЫ plum Unde liZa
chie Ы possum neq: 6o pauti quidm Zanza
tbЫaa Яanium znarum quam mihidir
natur intracipthnrater mete qЫ pe
ZЫbЯo mea na ut Ы connЫadonem taz
nitonendi 6oUalrane 7 conЫi mirabh
Conam omni naЯione qЫ Ыubommactio
q nЫ aluur dr nee umquam Ыuit nee aЫ
nee tuoЫ Ы pe dir paЯrem inЫuram
pЫ pncipio Ыquo 6omme pncipum oa
ZЫonem utЫmur 1 Ы Ыummhm xpm qui
cum paЫpe poika rimr Ыure Zstumir
aЫ Onienm yuЫuli Ыinue aЫ paЯrem
inЫnabilie zonium aЫ omne pncipui
yЫpum Ыicausintumbiha hominen
Ыm monte 6eonica 1ncelir 1 daЫuth om
pОЯЫamm yuromne nЫ aueЫ Ыr Яoi
ner dЫr 1n Ыnonum 7 ommr linna 7
Ыruae 6o q dЫr uЫr mЫr xpe quem 6maum:
1 6oЫpemamur Ыlumeum mor puЫma
lЫdar muonum aЫy: mortuonum qui pЫ
de umcuq: e Ыucta pua ierkrude 1nuob
hbunde Ыmpem donum 7 pizmur 1nmon
Ыaluceur qui Ыuet 6muu lubii roboaЫ muти
ut Ыne Ыlu dr 1conЫualer xpi quen conp
amun 7 Ыlomamir umumdm 1n Zhmza
te Ыlaur nommir yur de 6o xpe 1nuoca
me 1n die Zhbulationir cuе: 1lu habo te
1 maЫ mЫcalbу me

When a castle at the Hill of Mullaghmast in south Kildare was being demolished, this limestone boulder was found being re-used as a lintel. The spiral carvings, which are close in style to those found on metal dress-pins and brooches of the period, date it to the sixth century AD, after the mission of St Patrick. What is intriguing, however, is that its symbolism reminds us that in Ireland the arrival of Christianity did not mark a sudden break with the past. Instead, the stone speaks of a remarkable continuity of one of the so-called Celtic rituals that resonates even today: the sword in the stone.

The idea of the true king being the one who can pull a sword from a stone is central to the British legends of King Arthur. Conor Newman of NUI Galway has noted that many sacred stones that functioned as 'icons of tribal and cultural identity' have straight, narrow grooves on their surfaces. These marks have generally been dismissed as results of vandalism or ploughing. But Newman has pointed out that they occur far too often and are far too regular for this to be the case.

The Mullaghmast Stone is one such stone. It almost certainly stood at where the Uí Dúnlainge kings of Leinster were initiated. In itself, it is notable that such an important ritual object has no Christian symbolism. 'There is little doubt that this is the inaugural stone of the Uí Dúnlainge', says Newman, 'and there's nothing in the ornamentation that you could describe as Christian'. This does not necessarily mean that those who first used the stone were clinging to the old religion, but it does show that in Ireland, Christianity was often another layer on top of older traditions that survived and thrived. Rituals of kingship in particular retained their broad shape for another thousand years after the emergence of Christianity; the idea of the 'sword in the stone' seems to have lasted at least from the fifth or sixth centuries to the twelfth.

The Mullaghmast Stone has four blade marks on the left-hand side and two very deep ones on the top. The new king, it seems, would have struck or sharpened his sword against the stone as a key part of the inauguration ritual. The persistence of such rituals may be rooted in the paradox that emerging local chieftains, with new wealth gained from the exploitation of the collapse of Roman Britain, needed to disguise the novelty of their power. These *arrivistes*, says Newman, 'still have to legitimate their power. If you are an *arriviste*, the first thing you do is buy a house and fill it with antiques. There is a very keen awareness of the rituals surrounding that moment of taking your place in history'. These rituals may have been self-consciously archaic, used by upstarts to claim the authority of antiquity.

45

At the beginning of the nineteenth century, the last member of a branch of the Mulholland family, a schoolteacher about to die without heir, sent for his former pupil, the Belfast merchant Adam McLean. Having been instructed to dig at a certain spot in Mulholland's garden, McLean found this bell enclosed in the magnificently ornate shrine that was made for it in Armagh around 1100. The Mulholland family had been 'keepers of the bell' since mediaeval times.

Unlike so many of the objects featured in this book, the bell owes its power not to its finesse or opulence but to its simplicity. Small (less than seven inches high) and plain, it is made of two pieces of thick sheet-iron, coated in bronze, closely riveted together, with a little looped handle at the top. The tongue of the bell appears to be a later addition. It is it simplicity that made credible the belief that the bell belonged to St Patrick, even though it is probably of later origin. The *Annals of Ulster*, for 553, written many centuries after the event, record the opening of the tomb of St Patrick 60 years after his death and the recovery from it of his goblet, the 'Angel's Gospel' and the 'Bell of the Testament'. An angel allegedly directed St Colmcille (Columba) to send the cup to Down and the bell to Armagh, and to keep the Gospel himself.

The bell was certainly an object of great veneration in the Middle Ages, and was woven into the legends of Patrick's miraculous deeds. (He was said to have rung a bell at the conclusion of his apocalyptic battle against the forces of evil, disguised as birds, on Croagh Patrick.) Aside from its religious and legendary power, though, the bell had great political significance. Along with the *Book of Armagh* and the 'staff of Jesus' (destroyed in Dublin in the sixteenth century), the bell was crucial to Armagh's claim to be the centre of Patrick's legacy, and thus the superior seat of Irish Christianity.

The church was a new source of power and prestige in Ireland, and claims to primacy in church affairs were never going to be uncontested. As Patrick began to be accepted as the sole father of Irish Christianity, it was important to be able to prove a direct connection to his authority. Armagh, Downpatrick and Saul all claimed to be the site of his burial. Other centres disputed Armagh's primacy—the early partisan of Armagh's claims, Tírechán, complains of those who 'hate Patrick's territorial jurisdiction' and attack Armagh's status. Thus, however touching it may be as a plain expression of simple piety, the bell was also a mighty weapon in a struggle for power. From the earliest days, the spiritual message of the new religion could not be entirely disentangled from old-fashioned political struggles for pre-eminence.

100 WHERE TO SEE IT: NATIONAL MUSEUM OF IRELAND-ARCHAEOLOGY, KILDARE STREET, DUBLIN 2; 00-353-1-6777444; WWW.MUSEUM.IE

In 1913 a man cutting turf in Springmount bog in Ballyhutherland, Co. Antrim, found this set of six yew tablets, held together by leather straps. The inner tablets are hollowed out on both sides, forming the pages of a small wooden book. These inner surfaces are filled with wax, on which someone wrote, or rather literally inscribed with a pointed stylus, a biblical text.

This is the earliest extant Irish manuscript. Someone, a monk or a scholar at a monastic school, has written onto the wax in a beautifully precise hand parts of Psalms 30 and 31 from the Old Testament. What is fascinating is that the style of writing is already a distinctively Irish form ('Irish majuscule'), one which survived into modern times. In a manner typical of Irish culture, it combines elements of existing scripts in a new way. Literacy may be a cultural import from the post-Roman world, but from very early on it is being rooted in the local. There are later stories of wonderful manuscripts being written by sixth-century scribes and saints, and St Columba in particular is regularly described as 'writing in his hut'. Another saint's 'life' tells of a boy being sent 'so that he might learn the science of letters'. Not all of this early writing was religious. Linguistic evidence suggests that the task of writing down the voluminous texts of Brehon law began around this time too, but none of those manuscripts survives.

Literacy is not the same as learning. Reading and writing belonged to the new order of the Christian monasteries, but there was also an old order of learning in Ireland. The *filidh* (poets, savants and keepers of tribal lore) enjoyed enormous prestige and continued to assert their professional privileges. This is what makes early Irish literature so rich: the cross-fertilisation of the new Christian literacy with the old oral traditions of mythology and satire, lyric poetry and eulogies for local kings. As Celtic scholar Proinsias Mac Cana put it, 'By the end of the sixth century, the church (that is to say the monasteries) and the *filidh* had come to terms and from that time on there is evidence of an ever-increasing practical co-operation and assimilation between them'.

The result of this fusion is Western Europe's first non-Classical vernacular literature. Monks wrote in Irish as well as in Latin, and they wrote down old pre-Christian stories as well as religious texts. The metres of Latin hymns and the habit of rhyming crept into Irish poetry. The demands of writing made for new, more direct styles of expression, more easily understood by lay people than the often baroque and self-consciously elitist learning of the *filidh*. Literacy did not, however, obliterate what had gone before: to an extent that is practically unique to Ireland, it gave it a new and much longer life.

49

Found in the 1930s in a crannóg (lake dwelling) on the south side of Ballinderry Lough in Co. Offaly, this is one of the most startlingly complex objects ever discovered in Ireland. It arose from a richly sophisticated and cosmopolitan culture in which pre-Christian forms are being subtly re-shaped to elaborate Christian theology. It tells us that Irish art was both absorbing very complex iconography from as far away as Palestine and enriching it with older pagan symbolism. The brooch is zoomorphic (animal-shaped) and penannular (there is a gap in the ring); this is a style developed in Roman Britain but popular in Ireland between the fifth and seventh centuries. This is the most elaborate ever found. Its maker may have been an Irish artist-craftsman of inter-national standing, who may also have made the escutcheons of the largest hanging bowl found in one of the most famous archaeological discov-eries in western Europe, the Anglo-Saxon ship burial from Sutton Hoo in East Anglia.

The basic image is pre-Christian: the two-headed snake biting its own tail, a symbol of eternity and regeneration. This snake, here, is not a symbol of Satan. It hints, rather, at the resurrec-tion of Christ, the analogy being with the snake's ability to shed its skin and be 'reborn'. The key to understanding the Christian iconography of the brooch is found on what is known as the 'Marigold Stone', from Carndonagh, Co. Donegal. The two objects have the same pattern of a geo-metrical stem rising towards a marigold flower.

More remarkably, however, the patterns on the brooch come from Jerusalem, specifically from the jars of holy oil sold to wealthy pilgrims at the Church of the Holy Sepulchre, the reputed burial place of Jesus. Inscribed on some of these jars were the images that lie behind the patterns on the Ballinderry brooch. They show Christ's tomb under the dome of the church. Rising from the tomb is the Tree of Life on which Jesus ascends into Heaven. In Irish art, the face of Christ at the top of the tree is represented by a marigold. This is the image of the resurrection shown in abstract and condensed form on the back of the brooch. In addition, the millefiori cross on the brooch front represents the most famous monument to the resurrection in Jerusalem, the Crux Gemmata (jewelled cross).

'There is a remarkably sophisticated iconogra-phy at work here', says Conor Newman of NUI Galway, 'and it is the same message which ulti-mately can be sourced to the iconologists at work in Jerusalem in the sixth century. So you have a brooch that is pagan in its original form but that carries this complex symbolism of the resurrected Christ'. Very early in the history of Irish Christianity, there is a brilliant mixture of continuity with older traditions and up-to-date cosmopolitan thinking. 'You have somebody', says Newman, 'living around AD 600 in the midlands, whose brooch is probably made by the same person who made the biggest hanging bowl found at Sutton Hoo, and its iconography speaks not just to his religious per-suasion, but to deep intellectual traditions that are most current in Palestine at this time'.

52

This object, found on a riverbank at Donore, Co. Meath, in 1984, is almost certainly the handle for a church door. Its opulence and sophistication tell us how far Irish monasteries had come from the largely ascetic impulses behind their foundation. It reveals a period of obvious prosperity, in which the church is fully integrated in the structures of power. The handle is a spectacular and supremely confident expression of technological mastery. It is made up of three pieces: a beautifully engraved circular plate of tinned bronze, a splendid lion's head that was probably made from a wax model and a frame that was probably cast from a two-piece mould. The lion's eyes are inlaid with brown glass made to look like amber.

In addition to its technological sophistication, the handle's artistry is evidence of a confident cosmopolitanism. The lion's head obviously comes from Roman traditions (similar images were used in Roman temples) and from biblical iconography (the lion is often a symbol for the evangelist St Mark). More specifically, decoration on the head of this lion is comparable to some of the decoration in the Lindisfarne Gospels, the superb illuminated manuscript from Northumbria. Thus, Irish, Pictish, Romano-British and Anglo-Saxon influences are mingling to produce a vigorous stew of visual styles. The idea of the lion as doorkeeper is also a more broadly European image: it is found, for example, on the door of a chapel in the palace of the Frankish emperor Charlemagne at Aachen.

All of this is a far cry from the origins of monasticism in the deserts of North Africa and Asia Minor as a way of fleeing the entanglements of the ordinary world. This ascetic strain certainly survived in Ireland, most notably in the stark remoteness of the monastic settlement on Skellig Michael, off the Kerry coast, but there is nothing stark or remote about the Donore handle. It speaks instead of a worldly, cosmopolitan church with connections to both local politics and international currents. It is significant, indeed, that Irish monks seeking to attain the original monastic ideal of removal felt it necessary to go to the Skellig, or even, by the ninth century, to Iceland. The need to go to such literal extremes suggests an awareness that the mainstream monasteries were increasingly integral to the economic and political life of the country. They enjoyed the patronage of, and were intertwined with, the powerful local dynasties that were asserting control over an expanding and increasingly productive society. This was a period of great clearances of forests, of the expansion of arable land and of the building of perhaps as many as 50,000 ring-forts as enclosures for well-off farmers. The church was a key part of this expansive Ireland.

This was a church that had felt confident enough to engage in long disputes with Rome about the correct date for the most important Christian festival, Easter. It was now developing new ideas about pilgrimage and penance that had a profound influence on Christianity as a whole; and it was not embarrassed to display its wealth and sophistication on a church door.

55

It has been called the Irish equivalent of the Sistine Chapel, and the analogy is not ridiculous. The *Book of Kells* is not merely the greatest work of Irish visual art, it belongs among the great creations of Western art.

One big difference between the *Book of Kells* and the Sistine Chapel, however, is that the manuscript is also funny and playful and combines its grand religious vision with a homely humanity. Everywhere there are touches of comedy: a letter extended to form a monk's tonsure, a word broken in two by the paw of a cat. This is not to say that the task of making the book was anything but serious. It required the skin of 185 calves to make the vellum pages. The range of pigments used for its colours—orpiment, vermilion, verdigris, woad and, perhaps, folium—is far greater than that of other contemporary books. There may have been one guiding visionary leading the team of monks, as it is clear that on many pages the script and the images were created by the same hand.

There have long been arguments about where the book was made, with suggestions ranging from Spain to (more plausibly) the great monastery at Lindisfarne, in Northumbria. The consensus is that it was probably made on the island of Iona, off the west coast of Scotland, whose heavily Irish monastery was founded by St Colmcille in 563. It may well have been intended to honour his memory: from early on it was known as 'the great book of Columcille'. Iona was raided by Vikings in 802 and 806, and many of its monks retreated to a new base at Kells. The probability is that they brought at least the bulk of the book with them: some

subsequent work on it may have been done in this new monastery in Co. Meath.

Whatever its precise history, the book can be securely placed within Irish culture. The contorted animals, highly stylised humans and fabulously ornate initial lettering are rooted in the La Tène tradition of 'Celtic' art that by the ninth century had been alive in Ireland for 1,000 years. Many of the animal and bird images are comparable to those created by the great Irish metalworkers, but, in a way that is also typically Irish, the book is fed by many cultural streams, from Pictish sculpture in Scotland to Visigothic and Carolingian design in Spain and France, and even to the Coptic art of the North African church.

It seems that the monks who created the book paid more attention to the sumptuous visual art that decorates it than to the sacred text: there are numerous spelling mistakes, and at one point a whole page is repeated. This suggests that the book was never intended for practical use in readings at Mass, but rather was regarded from the beginning as an extraordinary object. The book's richness lies in what art historian Roger Stalley has called:

> the constant humour and vitality of the ornament, the freshness of the pigments, the unwavering beauty of the script and the haunting ambiguity of the religious imagery. Its genius is that it is sacred but never solemn. The vividness, vibrancy and constant, joyful invention make it seem almost a living thing.

WHERE TO SEE IT: OLD LIBRARY, TRINITY COLLEGE DUBLIN; 00-353-1-8962320; WWW.TCD.IE/LIBRARY/BOOKOFKELLS

Qui autem exaltauerit se humilia
bitur & quis humiliauerit exaltabi
tur

Uae autem uobis scribae & pha
rissaei hypochritae quiclau
otas regnum caelorum ante homi
nes uos autem nonintratis neque
uero euntes sinitis intrare

Uae uobis scribae & pharissaei
hypochritae quoniam comeditis
domus uiduarum occassione longe
orantes propter hoc accipietis
plus iudicium

Uae uobis scribae & pharissaei
hypochritae quiarcum tas
mare & aridam utfaciatis unum
prosilitum & cumfuerit factus

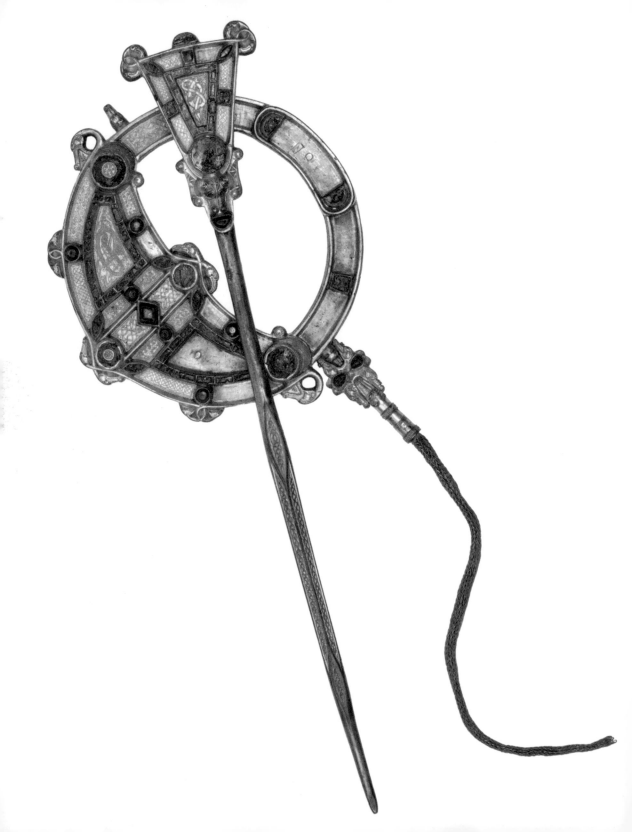

In the late-nineteenth century, copies of the 'Tara' brooch were a must-have item of Celtic chic. One important nationalist organisation, Inghinidhe na hÉireann (Daughters of Ireland), headed by Maud Gonne, adopted it as its membership badge. The brooch, made over a thousand years earlier, became a symbol of the Irish cultural revival because it presented a stunning answer to Victorian theories of Irish racial backwardness.

In this case, at least, the symbol is not let down by the reality: this brooch is an object that speaks of a culture functioning at the highest level of sophistication. It is not, in fact, associated with Tara: it was found in 1850 by a child playing on the seashore at Bettystown, Co. Meath, and sold by a 'poor woman' to a watchmaker in Drogheda. The watchmaker subsequently sold it to George Waterhouse, a shrewd Dublin businessman already involved in producing Celtic Revival jewellery, who renamed it the 'Tara' Brooch and displayed it at the Great Exhibition in London in 1851. Now, it seems not so much a museum piece as a whole museum in itself, a bravura display of multiple mastery. Although it is less than 9cm in diameter, approximately 76 patterns have been identified on its surface.

Both faces of the brooch, and even the inner and outer edges of the ring, are covered with a teeming profusion of designs, each executed with dazzling skill. Even the cord that secured the brooch in position culminates in an elaborately designed link that incorporates serpent, animal and human heads. It is not the expression of a particular technique; it is a virtuoso performance of virtually every technique known to late-seventh and early-eighth-century metalworkers. Gossamer-thin, interlocking spirals of copper-alloy are set against gold and silver. The technique of so-called chip-carving, borrowed from Germanic jewellery, is applied to create elongated birds, beasts and spiral patterns. Beaded and twisted gold wires are melded to bases of sheet gold. Variegated studs of glass and amber punctuate the patterns. On the front, a tiny filigree animal sits in a panel just 2cm wide, its front paw raised and its body winding back on itself. The back bears other animal patterns.

This brooch was made for a member of an elite that saw itself as the equal of any other in post-Roman Europe. The brooch was used to fasten a cloak, which was worn over a tunic; a form of power-dressing that ultimately derives from the Mediterranean and the fashions of high-ranking officials in Byzantium. In Ireland, brooches were used in this way by high-status women, as well as by men, clerics and secular rulers alike. In slightly later high crosses, even Jesus and the Virgin Mary are wearing 'Tara'-type brooches.

The brooch also resonates with pre-Christian Irish beliefs. In one tale from around the time the 'Tara' brooch was made, a Munster king who sleeps with the goddess of sovereignty tells his wife to clothe the goddess in a purple cloak and 'the queen's brooch'. What we see in the 'Tara' brooch is a native Irish elite at the height of its self-confidence, easily integrating Christian with pre-Christian traditions, and its local power with a sense of being European. It is arguably the last time that such ease would be possible.

WHERE TO SEE IT: NATIONAL MUSEUM OF IRELAND-ARCHAEOLOGY, KILDARE STREET, DUBLIN 2; 00-353-1-6777444; WWW.MUSEUM.IE

It was found in 1868, under a stone slab in a ring-fort in Reerasta, near Ardagh, Co. Limerick, with a second, plainer bronze chalice and four gilt silver brooches. Along with the Derrynaflan chalice, this is one of the finest liturgical vessels of the Early Christian world. Its beauty lies in the contrast between the plain sheen of the polished silver and the finesse and complexity of the ornamentation: gold filigree of stylised birds and beasts; interlace in filigree and other techniques; intricate studs of red, blue and yellow glass (sometimes multi-coloured or topped by filigree); and beautifully engraved lettering that spells out the names of the Apostles, with Paul being substituted for Judas. Like so much else from this extraordinary period, the chalice suggests a culture that is at once international and insular.

'The model', says Raghnall Ó Floinn of the National Museum, 'is Late Roman tableware, from the early centuries AD. It has parallels not in Western Europe but with Byzantine vessels now in St Mark's in Venice—not because there is direct Eastern influence but because they both draw on a common Roman ancestor'. The squat shape of the two-handled bowl of the chalice, however, is indigenously Irish, and the animal art, with its typical abstraction, is very different from the more realistic Roman style of representation.

This Irish love of complexity is everywhere on the Ardagh chalice. Numbers play a large part in the design: the Apostles are echoed in the twelve studs and twelve panels of the band at the top. What is extraordinary, though, is the number of pieces that make up the chalice: more than 350.

The skill and complexity lavished on objects such as this highlight something conspicuous only by its absence. From this golden age of Irish Christianity, there are few surviving churches.

The simple stone oratories that do survive are not at all typical of the general run of contemporary Irish churches. Stone endures, wood perishes —and most churches in Ireland were wooden. A poem in the exuberant monkish collection *Hisperica Famina* describes a 'wooden oratory… fashioned out of candle-shaped beams' and talks of how monks would 'hew the sacred oaks with axes, in order to fashion square chapels'. The usual word for a church in early mediaeval Irish is *dairthech*, literally, 'oak house'.

These buildings were rectangular and probably plain. So, even while the Irish were making religious objects of astonishing opulence, they were using them in relatively humble spaces. The explanation for the tendency to use wood in church building is certainly not to be found in a lack of skill in masonry—as Ireland's elaborate stone high crosses attest. One possibility, hinted at in the mention of the 'sacred oaks', is that Ireland retained a pre-Christian attachment to the holiness of trees.

The effect of this traditionalism could well have been to make the objects contained in these churches all the more striking. The author of the *Hisperica Famina* concluded his description by remarking 'the chapel contains innumerable objects, which I shall not struggle to unroll from my wheel of words'. It is hard to imagine that however innumerable these objects, any was more magnificent than the Ardagh chalice.

100 WHERE TO SEE IT: NATIONAL MUSEUM OF IRELAND-ARCHAEOLOGY, KILDARE STREET, DUBLIN 2; 00-353-1-6777444; WWW.MUSEUM.IE

This is the most spectacular item from the hoard of eucharistic vessels found in a shallow hole at an ancient church site, Derrynaflan, in Co. Tipperary, in 1980. Although the chalice and strainer found with it are fine objects, the paten is of an altogether higher order. It tells us a great deal about the Irish elite of its time. The paten is a large, silver dish, with a diameter of approximately 37cm, probably intended to hold the sacred host during Mass. (It is unlikely to have been used regularly, and may have been intended purely as a votive offering.) As with the Ardagh chalice, the sheen of the silver sets off an extravagant, polychromatic display of ornament, set in twelve sections around the circumference and on the rim. Gold filigree and finely knitted wires of silver form dizzying patterns on panels studded with imitation gemstones made of cast glass and held in copper-alloy frames.

Exquisitely traced golden men squat back to back in a tiny panel. Snakes, stags and eagles twist and rear in minute spaces. As with so much else from this zenith of early Irish art, the paten is a local response to a European model—in this case, Late Roman silver platters that were decorated with animals around the rim. This desire for a connection to the old Roman world is essentially aristocratic. The paten is also elitist in a theological sense: the images contain symbolic references to redemption, the Eucharist, baptism and beasts from the Book of Genesis and the psalms, but these symbols would be apparent only to the educated few.

Which raises the question: for whom was this elite object made? Derrynaflan was patronised by Feldmid Mac Crimthainn. 'The betting', says Raghnall Ó Floinn of the National Museum, 'is that he was the man who actually had the paten commissioned'. Feldmid, more than anyone else at this time, embodies the intertwining of religious and secular power. He was both king of Munster and a senior ecclesiastic. He claimed the high kingship of Ireland between 820 and 847 (although he never actually held it), while retaining his church offices, which came to include the abbotships of Cork and Clonfert. This was not unusual in contemporary Europe, but in Feidlimid's case its contradictions were especially stark.

Feldmid appears in the annals in different guises. His forces assaulted and burned the monasteries of Gallen and Fore in 822 and 830, respectively, and attacked Kildare in 836—all, presumably, to further his claim to the high kingship. Yet, he is also recorded as an ascetic anchorite, as a scribe and even, posthumously, as a saint. He was a terror, but, it seems, a holy terror. Feldmid's aggression was evidence that a long peace between the major regional factions that dominated Irish politics—the Uí Néill overlords of Tara, the Éoganachta (Feldmid's dynasty in Munster) and the Connachta in the west—was coming to an end even before external shocks began to have a profound effect. His possible role in commissioning the Derrynaflan paten is a reminder that these heavenly objects were not free from earthly connections.

65

Objects such as the Ardagh chalice or the Derrynaflan paten are obviously very special. They belonged to a social and ecclesiastical elite and were used rarely, if at all. What was ordinary religion like? How did most people interact with the world of the saints? This unique shrine gives us some sense of popular faith and ritual in eighth-century Ireland.

The shrine, discovered by turfcutters in a bog in Co. Sligo, is made up of four hinged, copper-alloy plates, each enclosing a fragment of a simple leather belt. The belt clearly belonged to a popular early saint. The bog at Moylough where it was found is not far from the site of an early monastery at Carrowntemple, so there may well be a connection to this holy place. The shrine is it-self in the form of a belt: the two front plates form a false 'buckle' whose frames are decorated with bird and animal heads and end in elaborate glass pieces. The overall impression is somewhat dulled now: originally, the belt would have been a riot of colour, with shiny silver panels, blue and white glass studs, and red and yellow enamel borders.

What is particularly interesting about the shrine, however, is that it was not kept in some monastic treasury, away from the ordinary believers. The patterns of wear on its surfaces show that it was much used. What was it used for? Miracles and blessings. There is something very intimate in the way this relic was deployed. The hinges and the wear and tear show that it was actually placed around the bodies of devotees. Monks themselves regarded the belts of their holy predecessors as a form of spiritual protection. One Irish monk in Austria wrote that 'the girdle of Finnan' protected him 'against disease, against anxiety, against the charms of foolish women'. Presumably, the devotee hoped to gain this same protection, at least against the first of these evils.

Saints' belts even acquired a frankly magical aura. In a Scots Gaelic legend, the hero MacUalraig uses the 'magic belt of Saint Fillan' to capture a water nymph. The Moylough belt shrine was probably placed around the bodies of supplicants who came with all sorts of illnesses, wounds and defor-mities. There is a particularly strong early-mediaeval tradition in Western Europe of the belts or girdles of saints being placed around the waist of a woman undergoing a difficult childbirth. There are later records of the purported girdles of Ss Joseph, Margaret of Antioch, Brigid and many others being used in this way.

The elaborate nature of the Moylough shrine makes it highly unlikely that it was actually used for women in labour, but it may have been placed on pregnant women as a blessing to en-sure safe childbirth. It reminds us that, for all the sophistication of early Irish Christianity, for most people religion still functioned as it always had, as a way of trying to control an unpredictable and often frightening world.

100 WHERE TO SEE IT: NATIONAL MUSEUM OF IRELAND-ARCHAEOLOGY, KILDARE STREET, DUBLIN 2; 00-353-1-6777444; WWW.MUSEUM.IE

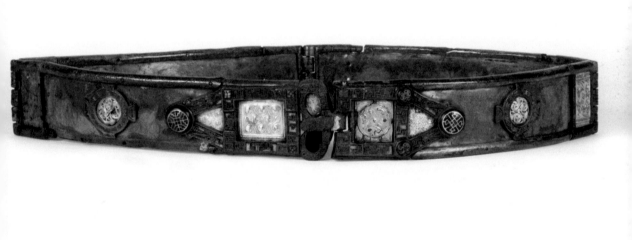

At first glance, this plaque, made from a thin sheet of copper-alloy and originally attached to some kind of wooden or metal backing, could be from anywhere in early mediaeval Europe. It is Christ on the cross. An angel hovers on each side of his head; on the left side is the Roman soldier who offered Jesus a sponge soaked in vinegar; on the right is the soldier who stabbed his side with a lance. This iconography had been used in Europe for about 200 years before this piece was made in Ireland.

The plaque, found in St John's churchyard on the shores of Lough Ree, in Rinnagan, Co. Roscommon, and originally a much shinier, more gilded object than it is now, is intriguing in two ways. First, what looks to us like a standard image is actually very rare in the Ireland of this time. The most striking aspect of Irish art of this period is that it displays relatively little interest in showing the human form or using images to tell stories. It is not that Irish artists could not deal with human figures—they did so on high crosses—they simply chose not to do it very often. They, and presumably their patrons, were more interested in the fantastical filigrees and mind-bending patterns at which they excelled to a degree unsurpassed in Europe.

The Rinnagan Crucifixion is thus, says Raghnall Ó Floinn of the National Museum, 'the only narrative scene of such an early date that we have. There are fragments of other objects that may have been similar, but they are very much in the minority'. Apart from its rarity, the other startling thing about this Crucifixion is how utterly Irish it is. The basic image may be standard across Christendom, but the way it is treated is distinctive. If you look at it at all closely, what emerges is not just an object of Christian worship, but an eloquent statement of the way the Irish made their own synthesis of Christianity and an older culture. Christ's mask-like face is full-frontal, with an implacable stare that is oddly familiar from the pre-Christian Corleck Head, perhaps 600 years earlier. Jesus is not dead here: his eyes are open, and the image is meant to be triumphant. Even more fascinating is the pattern on Christ's chest. It looks nothing like the standard image of the Crucifixion. Rather, it is made to look like a breastplate, with three back-to-back C-shaped scrolls. There are similar patterns of triple spirals above the head of Christ and on the wings of the angels—a triple triad. This is typical Irish imagery, again going back to the Iron Age, and beyond. Even Jesus, it seems, is more than a little bit Irish.

69

When hurlers and Gaelic footballers describe their ultimate ambition, they often use a simple shorthand: 'a Celtic cross'. Since the late-nineteenth century, the Gaelic Athletic Association has used a high cross for its logo and for All-Ireland medals. The modern use of the cross as a symbol of Irish achievement dates to at least the 1853 Irish Industrial Exhibition, in Dublin, which displayed high crosses as 'fine monuments of the artistic skill and devoted piety of our Celtic ancestors'.

The crosses are so deeply embedded in the Irish imagination that it seems almost sacrilegious to ask why they were made in the first place. There was no native tradition of building in cut stone, so the appearance of high crosses in the eighth century was a major cultural innovation. So, as we have seen, was the idea of depicting, in a relatively realistic way, human subjects and stories. The crosses are not widely evident beyond Ireland and Irish-influenced Scotland. They required a huge investment of skill and resources and, as art historian Roger Stalley has put it, 'it is hard to believe they were undertaken for purely altruistic or religious motives'. Yet they were erected on a very large scale: about 300 of them survive, of which 100 are decorated with carved images.

The crosses undoubtedly served as gathering places for prayers for monks and pilgrims, but their scale and complexity far exceed this basic function. This cross, from Monasterboice in Co. Louth, is almost seven metres tall, and every available face is covered with elaborate carvings of a dazzling variety of scenes. The east face alone has Christ saving Peter from the water; Joshua; St Anthony tempted by demons; St Paul and St Anthony killing a devil; an angel shielding three children in the fiery furnace; and images of Elijah, Moses, Abraham and Isaac, David and Goliath, and David (again) killing a lion.

Some crosses are inscribed with the names of kings or abbots, suggesting that they acted as potent symbols of the power and status of these dignitaries. Part of their function is to claim territory and mark boundaries. It is striking in this regard that the crosses are highly individual, with distinctive styles associated with different regions. The basic form is common to them all: a pyramidal base, a rectangular shaft culminating in a capstone and a large circle enclosing the arms of the cross. This circle may be intended to represent a halo around the figure of Christ, but it can also be seen as a cosmic symbol, in the manner of older Irish traditions of representations of the sun.

One way of looking at the crosses is that they represent a new assertion of biblical Christianity in the face of a new pagan threat. By the time the cross-builders were at their most active, that threat was all too real.

WHERE TO SEE IT: MONASTERBOICE, DROGHEDA, CO. LOUTH; 00-353-41-9872843

Very few objects ever did so much to change the course of Irish history as the fearsome and beautiful Viking longship. In the later-eighth century, Danish and Norwegian shipbuilders developed existing techniques to create vessels that could both traverse the high seas and navigate the great rivers of Europe. The longship was the spacecraft of its day, propelling adventurers across vast and hitherto unimaginable distances. In one raid in 858, a group sailed from Scandinavia to the coast of Spain, into the Mediterranean, on to Italy, up the River Rhône, raiding all the way; and they then sailed home.

The Vikings did not invent the techniques that made possible these light, fast ships, but they did perfect them. The method involved splitting oak trunks with axes, chisels and wedges into long, thin and remarkably flexible planks. These were fixed with iron nails to a single sturdy keel and then to each other, with one plank overlapping the next to create the distinctive clinker effect. The low, sleek shape made the ships highly manoeuvrable when steered with a single rudder mounted on the right-hand side of the stern. (This is why the right-hand side of a ship, and now also of an aeroplane, is known as the starboard—i.e. steerboard—side.) The ship's shallow draught meant that it could be rowed far upriver into the heart of Europe—or, in the case of Ireland, of the island.

Built c.815, shortly after the Viking raids on Ireland began, the Oseberg ship is more than 22m long and 5m wide. Unlike earlier vessels, which had rowlocks on the gunwale, it has fifteen pairs of oar ports, placed low down so that the oars could strike the water at an efficient angle. Either rowed or sailed (the sail would have covered 90 sq m), it could reach a speed of 10 knots. It is preserved because it was used in 834 to inter a high-status woman in the Oseberg burial mound near the ancient town of Tønsberg in Norway. (Some objects of Irish decorated enamel were found with the burial, perhaps suggesting that the ship's owners were involved in raids on Ireland.) The prow and the stern, which rise in beautiful curves 5m above the waterline, have carvings of intertwined beasts, whose quality suggest this may have been a royal vessel. The image on the prow is not the dragon so beloved by filmmakers, but a serpent, whose tail is represented in the stern.

It is unlikely that the ships that first raided Irish coasts were anything as fine as the Oseberg vessel, which in any case would not have been rugged enough for the high seas. The general design, however, would have been the same—and that design took Scandinavian raiders and traders as far west as North America and farther east than Kiev. Yet, even with these masterpieces of functional beauty at their command, the Vikings still had to face into the unknown. Even 600 years after the Oseberg ship was built, an Icelandic navigational manual gives directions to Greenland: 'Turn left at the middle of Norway, keep so far north of Shetland that you can only see it if the visibility is very good, and far enough south of the Faroes that the sea appears halfway up the mountain slopes'. These voyages demanded not just great ships, but intrepid sailors.

73

This is one of the finest surviving examples of a technology that helped to transform Ireland in the ninth and tenth centuries: a Viking sword. With its cutting edge almost perfectly preserved in some places, it retains the ferocity that helped to make the Scandinavian warrior such a formidable force. Swords like this did not just allow the Vikings to ravage parts of Ireland; they forced indigenous Irish rulers to adapt to the demands of new warfare.

The Vikings typically imported their blades from high-quality workshops in the territory of the Frankish empire (today's Germany). The blade of the Ballinderry sword has a maker's name inlaid on it: Ulfberht. This identifies it as the work of a master, probably based in the Rhineland, whose blades have been found as far away as Russia. Over 150 of these blades have been discovered, suggesting that this was the early equivalent of a brand name, with an international cachet. There is even evidence of a division between genuine Ulfberht blades and cheaper forgeries; an early mediaeval case of brand piracy.

While the blade may have been imported, the hilt and pommel were made in Scandinavia. This one is particularly fine, decorated with hammered silver and carefully inscribed with lettering and abstract patterns. The upper side bears the name Hiltipreht, which may connect it to a Norwegian craftsman of that name. There is little doubt that this is a very high-status object that came to Ireland with the Vikings.

What is fascinating is where the sword was found in 1928: on the site of a crannóg, or lake dwelling, at Ballinderry, near Moate,

Co. Westmeath. It was found with other Viking objects—a longbow, two spearheads, an axehead and a gaming board—but a crannóg is a distinctively Irish form of dwelling. 'Crannógs are such an Irish type', says Andy Halpin of the National Museum, 'that it is very hard to believe this was a Viking site. So the best interpretation is that you are looking at an Irish chieftain or petty king who is wealthy enough to equip himself with the best of weaponry'.

> He is obviously in contact with Viking Dublin, or Limerick, which is not surprising because we know that, for this east midlands area, there was huge trade going back and forth. This sword symbolises, in a way, the long-term impact of the Vikings. If you are an Irish king and you have the Vikings on your doorstep, you need to get your act together. You need to have this sort of weaponry, but in order to have it, you need to be able to buy it, which means changing to an economic system that generates cash.

This arms race did not just affect the relationship between the Irish kings and the Scandinavian newcomers. It also set off a Darwinian struggle among the Irish themselves. The kings who could adapt to the Viking threat by acquiring the new technology could also compete more successfully against local rivals. Even more than their direct impact, which was shocking but relatively limited, it was these indirect effects that made the Vikings a catalyst for the transformation of Ireland.

100 WHERE TO SEE IT: NATIONAL MUSEUM OF IRELAND-ARCHAEOLOGY, KILDARE STREET, DUBLIN 2; 00-353-1-6777444; WWW.MUSEUM.IE

These weights were discovered in 1866 in a Viking grave at Islandbridge, just west of the centre of Dublin, and were first described by Oscar Wilde's father, Sir William Wilde. They are pretty objects. Some are topped with gilt-bronze discs that were reused from stolen ecclesiastical metalwork, and others are trimmed with blue glass. The most impressive is in the form of a gilt-bronze animal head, with intricate decoration. The point of the objects, however, is practical, not decorative. They are multiples of the same weight unit (26.6g), which, as Dr Pat Wallace, former director of the National Museum, figured out, was the standard unit used in Viking Dublin. (That unit was slightly different from those used elsewhere in the Scandinavian world.)

What we see in these little objects is what can reasonably be called the beginning of capitalism in Ireland. 'It's all about weighing silver', says Wallace. 'It is from this process that we eventually get our first coinage in Ireland, in 997. This is the beginning of that: you are a merchant, I am a merchant, we are doing a deal. We both have a weighing scales. We do the deal in silver, and we have a lead weight to make sure we are not cheating each other'. The Vikings used 'hack silver'—cut-off bits of silver objects—as a kind of small change. They used the metal for arm and neck rings that functioned both as practical, portable wealth and as status symbols: literally, flashing the cash.

It is unclear whether weights were used in Ireland before the Vikings: none has been found, but linguistic evidence suggests that they were known. What is certain, though, is that the Vikings brought with them the idea of an internationally tradable currency. In the ninth and tenth centuries they flooded Ireland with huge quantities of silver, which was the basis for their whole monetary system. Some of it originated in raiding (the known haul of silver from Viking raids on Frankish territory in the ninth century alone is 20 tonnes). Much of it came from trading with the Islamic world. It originated in central Asia, was brought to the great Arab cities where it was minted and thence sent, as payment for trade goods, up the Russian rivers and on to Sweden. This shiny metal is thus a tangible form of a wave of economic globalisation breaking over Northwest Europe, including Ireland.

A system of standard weights implies a lot more than increased trade. Someone has to set the standards and to police them. Tighter political control of this kind is possible in towns, and Dublin became the largest urban centre in Viking Ireland. It was founded first in the 840s as a *longphort*, a base for ships and raiding parties; and then, more permanently, as a defended town or *dún* around 917.

It is possible that the original *longphort* was at Islandbridge, although more recent evidence suggests it may have been at what is now South Great George's Street, and while it seems probable that the *longphort* and Viking town were co-extensive, what is clear from the weights is that Viking merchants had a presence in the Dublin area even before it emerged as a fully fledged town. They were pioneers of the Irish market economy.

WHERE TO SEE THEM: NATIONAL MUSEUM OF IRELAND-ARCHAEOLOGY, KILDARE STREET, DUBLIN 2; 00-353-1-6777444; WWW.MUSEUM.IE

38. ROSCREA BROOCH, LATE-NINTH CENTURY

It may not be as spectacular as some of the great brooches from eighth-century Ireland, but there are two important things about this beautiful piece of metalwork found near Roscrea, Co. Tipperary. It is distinctively Irish; and it could not have been made without the Vikings.

About a century after the Scandinavian raiders began to appear as terrifying intruders, we have an object that tells a story of cultural integration. The Viking presence in Ireland was not an easy one, but Irish culture was good at absorbing influences and remaking them, even when they came in the form of an initial violent shock. The imprint of the invaders on Irish metalwork is obvious. First, there is the basic material: high-quality silver. Good silver had been rare in Ireland, where it was used sparingly and for highly prized objects. The Vikings had access to vast quantities of the metal. Through trading, Irish craftsmen got access to lots of silver. There is another imported material that is obvious in the Roscrea brooch: the settings are made of amber from the shores of the Baltic Sea. Previously, these features on an Irish brooch would have been made of coloured glass or enamel.

Yet, for all the silver and amber, no one would have had any difficulty identifying this as an Irish object. The gold filigree work on the brooch, albeit cruder than appears on its predecessors, is clearly mimicking older, more sophisticated Irish work. The abstract patterns and elongated animals are typical of the basic forms of Irish visual art. There is as much continuity here as there is innovation.

The fact that Irish craftsmen are using Viking materials and influences (and, more importantly, that their Irish patrons are comfortable with them doing so) tells us that the Viking invasions were traumatic but not catastrophic. They did not destroy native Irish power. They did not trigger a 'nationalist' response in which the Irish banded together to drive out the foreigner. They did not produce a cultural reaction of seeking to emphasise the purity of indigenous traditions in the face of new challenges. Instead, Irish rulers competed with the Scandinavians when they could, attacked them when they were vulnerable, traded with them when it was profitable to do so and extorted money from them when the opportunity arose. They also used them as military allies in their continuing conflicts with rival Irish dynasties. As early as 850, the king of North Brega, Cináed Mac Conaing, attacked the Uí Néill and ravaged their lands in conjunction with the Norse. As a reminder that the Vikings did not invent violent raiding, Cináed burned a church with 260 refugees inside. The Roscrea brooch tells us that there were more creative cross-fertilisations of the cultures as well.

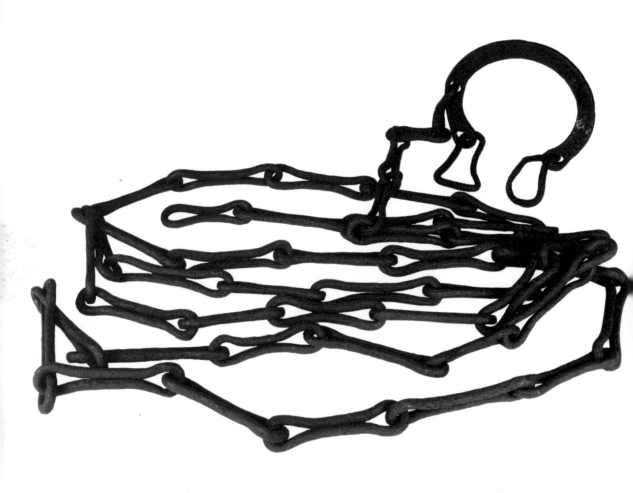

The clink of this iron chain is a dark note that sounds through much of Irish history, from St Patrick to twentieth-century institutions of incarceration. It is the sound of slavery. It was found, along with a human skull, iron spearhead and bronze pin, near Ardakillen crannóg, Co. Roscommon. Its function was brutally plain: to turn people into moveable property. It is a remnant of a trade that sold Irish slaves to places as far apart as Iceland and the Arab world.

The Old Norse word for a slave, 'thræll', is still part of our language, as thrall; but slavery had a long and disreputable history in Ireland before the Vikings. St Patrick was captured as a slave, and one of the first written documents in Irish history is his Letter to Coroticus, denouncing a British chieftain who had enslaved some members of his Christian flock. Bondage remained a feature of later Irish society: there are records in the annals of families selling children in times of need.

In the ninth century, Viking Dublin had emerged as a major slaving centre, from which captives, not merely from the rest of Ireland but also from Britain, were traded. The slave trade retained a significant role in the city's commerce until the twelfth century. (In a foretaste of nineteenth-century imperial rhetoric, the suppression of the slave trade was one excuse for the imposition of English overlordship in Ireland. The Anglo-Normans did in fact ban the use of Christian slaves; a progressive move that took several hundred years to disseminate across the rest of the European continent.)

Most slaves are anonymous, but we have the names of a few Irish people enslaved by Vikings. The 'Life' of St Findan (or Fintan), a Leinster monk who died in Switzerland in 878, records the capture of his sister by Vikings. When Findan seeks to ransom her, he himself is captured. He is sold in succession to four different masters before he escapes. There is specific mention of the enslaved Findan being bound in chains. The Icelandic *Laxdæla saga* contains the story of Melkorka (probably Máel Curcaig), the daughter of an Irish king, who is captured in a raid when she is just fifteen and sold in a slave market in Norway to 'Gilli the Russian'. She is then bought by a Viking called Höskuldr for 'three silver pieces'. He takes her to Iceland, where she bears him a son, Oláfr, whom she teaches to speak Irish. She somehow retains a defiant personality: when Höskuld's wife contemptuously flings stockings at her head, Melkorka responds by giving her a bloody nose. Few Irish slaves were the children of kings, and few would have survived such defiance. In the saga, Melkorka pretends for years to be deaf and dumb. Slaves, indeed, seldom get to speak or to leave the records of their own voices. The only sound they leave behind is the dull clank of a chain.

81

The slave chain is at the brutal end of the spectrum of Viking Ireland. This gorgeous cone of woven silver wire is, physically and symbolically, at the other extreme. It sits in the palm of the hand as lightly as a confection of spun sugar. It speaks of delicacy and delight, of complex conception and marvellous execution. It is hard to think of anything further removed from the idea of brute force.

'When I look at this', says Andy Halpin of the National Museum, 'the first question that comes to my mind is, How do you make it? From a technological point of view, it is an extraordinary thing'. There are three separate interwoven bands of silver, each composed of between fifteen and eighteen wires. Yet, Halpin says, it is very hard to find where any of these wires ends. The visual effect is that of a single thread turning endlessly around itself. There are traces of some kind of organic material inside the cone, possibly a wax shape around which the wires were woven. The visual imagination and the physical deftness required to do so are of the highest order.

This cone is one of the largest of a group of eighteen found in 1999 in the limestone cave at Dunmore, just north of Kilkenny city. The cave was well-known in early mediaeval Ireland, and the annals refer to a great slaughter perpetrated there around 930. The cones were found with coins that indicate a later date for their deposition—about 970.

The larger cones like the one pictured are unique objects, but the smaller ones in the hoard have parallels in Viking burials on the Isle of Man and Iceland. What we may have, then, is a development in Ireland of a general Norse form. The possibility that the cones were made in Dublin points to a very high level of distinctive craftsmanship in the new town by the mid-tenth century.

What were the cones for? A border of silver wire to which they seem originally to have been attached was found with the cones. More exciting was a small, unpromising-looking remnant of textile that turned out to be very fine silk. It seems that this was an elaborate silk garment with a silver wire border and cones that functioned either as tassels or as buttons. The silk itself may have been more valuable than all the silver put together. It had come, almost certainly, from either the Byzantine empire or the Arab world. The dye used to colour it was either red or purple. If it were the latter, the dress was truly amazing: purple dye was breathtakingly expensive. Either way, the woman who originally wore this garment must have made a dazzling spectacle. For the display of female wealth and status in tenth-century Western Europe, glamour does not get much more fabulous than this.

Who this woman was is as mysterious as the presence of this extraordinary example of Viking power-dressing in Co. Kilkenny. All we know is that someone had a garment worth a king's ransom, shoved it in a crack in a cave, perhaps in a moment of panic, and never came back for it.

100 WHERE TO SEE IT: NATIONAL MUSEUM OF IRELAND-ARCHAEOLOGY, KILDARE STREET, DUBLIN 2; 00-353-1-6777444; WWW.MUSEUM.IE

41. CARVED CROOK, EARLY-ELEVENTH CENTURY

For a long time the Viking intervention in Ireland was an unsettled affair. The invaders suffered some serious military reverses. Groups of raiders moved back and forth between Ireland, Britain and the continent. The development of Dublin was shaped by these patterns. In 902 the Viking leaders were expelled from the town and withdrew to north-western Britain. In 914, however, a large Norse fleet appeared off Waterford, having sailed from Brittany, and began making raids. Three years later this fleet was followed by Sitric Cáech, a grandson of King Ivár, whose dynasty had ruled in Dublin before 902. Sitric re-established control over Dublin while his brother Ragnall took control of Viking York. After Ragnall's death, Sitric ruled the joint kingdom, combining Dublin and York.

In 954 the expulsion of Eric Bloodaxe from York severed the connection between the two towns. Dublin became the main urban centre not just of the Irish Sea, but of the western Vikings. Dublin was clearly highly conscious of its place in the Viking maritime world: some of the loveliest items found there are toy ships, and there are also timbers with beautifully etched pictures of Norse ships complete with masts, sails and rigging. The town, as it settled down, began to develop its own culture, one that can reasonably be called Hiberno-Norse.

Dublin was a mixed space, in terms of both culture and population. Some items of personal ornamentation, such as oval brooches typical of Scandinavian women, have been found in Ireland, but Dr Pat Wallace, former director of the National Museum, who led the excavations of the Viking Dublin settlements, points out that in none of the Dublin excavations have typically Scandinavian items of female personal ornamentation ever turned up. His conclusion is that the female population of the town was almost entirely Irish. 'From a female point of view, it is a very Irish place', he says. This makes it probable that Irish was spoken, alongside Norse, in Dublin, resulting in a pidgin 'a bit like Hong Kong English'.

Norse words (especially commercial and maritime terms) seeped into the indigenous language. This mixing meant that the town quickly acquired its own culture, which is well represented in this beautifully carved wooden crook, found during the Museum's excavations at Fishamble Street. It is recognisably influenced by the Ringerike style, named after the district of Norway where it flourished. Ringerike, says Wallace, 'was not particularly popular in England, but it caught on here, and the Irish Vikings turned it into their own expression, particularly in Dublin'. The purpose of the carved crook is unclear. It may have been a whip handle or a furniture finial. There seems to have been a concentration of wood-turners and coopers in Fishamble Street. It was there that what James Lang called the 'Dublin school' of wood-craft had its centre.

100 WHERE TO SEE IT: NATIONAL MUSEUM OF IRELAND-ARCHAEOLOGY, KILDARE STREET, DUBLIN 2; 00-353-1-6777444; WWW.MUSEUM.IE

The Breac Maodhóg (the 'speckled or variegated shrine of St Maodhóg', a bishop and patron saint of the kings of Leinster) is a house-shaped reliquary, probably made in the late-eleventh century. It is made of large sheets of bronze that formed the background to its real glory: the delightful bronze plaques depicting lively figures of clerics and women. The bronze figures are, as Dr Pat Wallace puts it, 'so deeply moulded that it looks as if it is carved wood'.

The shrine is strongly associated with Drumlane, Co. Cavan. It was bought in the early 1840s by the antiquarian George Petrie, from 'Mr Reilly, a jeweller, a Cavan man'. The shrine speaks of continuity. Its shape is an enlargement of a form used since the eighth century, long before the Vikings. The clerics depicted

on the shrine are hardly ascetic. With their fine cloaks and tunics, long ringlets and extravagant beards, all worn in idiosyncratic styles, they seem every bit as fashion-conscious as the women. The curved ornamentation of the folds of the clerics' garments and the serpentine elaborations of their coiffure recall the traditional styles of Irish abstract art, but the figures are so lifelike and vividly individual that it does not seem too much of a stretch to think of them as partial portraits. Certainly the artist, in depicting a melancholy cleric with his head resting on his hand, his eyes drooping, was drawing not just on stylised forms but also on ob-

served human behaviour. On one end of the shrine there is a unique depiction of a musician playing a recognisably Irish harp—the oldest image of what would, much later, become a national symbol.

What is striking about these images is not just what they show but also what they do not. The luxury, humour and personality of the portraits suggest a church at ease in its cultural environment. There is none of the exaggerated triumphalism you get from a culture that has to shout to be heard, no sense of pressure or embattlement; this absence tells its own story. The Vikings came to Ireland with their own sophisticated religious mythology and belief systems. Initially, they were a threat to the established order in Ireland, not just as violent raiders but, specifically, as pagans. The second of these threats gradually faded along with the first. The Irish annals refer to the Scandinavians as *genti* or *geinte* (gentiles, pagans) until the second half of the ninth century, but the last mention of the 'heathens of Dublin' is in 942. There does not seem to have been any single moment of conversion, and there was probably a considerable overlap between those who had gone native and those who kept to the old religion. Conversion, as Donnchadh Ó Corráin has put it, 'must have come gradually, as an effect of assimilation'.

WHERE TO SEE IT: NATIONAL MUSEUM OF IRELAND-ARCHAEOLOGY, KILDARE STREET, DUBLIN 2; 00-353-1-6777444; WWW.MUSEUM.IE

Earlier in this book we saw a carved wooden crook from Viking Dublin. Its similarity to this gorgeous abbot's crozier from the great monastery of Clonmacnoise, Co. Offaly, is striking. Nothing could provide a more powerful visual contradiction of the old notion that the Vikings were simply an alien presence in Ireland, driven away by Brian Bóruma (Boru) in 1014 at the Battle of Clontarf. The crozier is probably associated with the shrine of the monastery's founder, Saint Ciarán. (Ciarán is recorded as appearing hundreds of years after his death to smite a would-be raider with his crozier.)

The crest of the crook has a series of animals apparently biting each other, but the most evocative aspect of the decoration is the snake-like animals in figure-of-eight patterns that decorate the sides. They are in a similar Ringerike-type style to that used for the wooden crook. Moreover, excavations at High Street in Dublin have unearthed bone trial pieces in which similar patterns have been practised by craftsmen. The likelihood is, therefore, that this crozier, a sacred Irish object dedicated to an ancient saint, was made in Dublin.

If this seems surprising, it is only because of the power of the story created by his followers of Brian as the hammer of the Vikings, who freed Ireland from a terrible curse. Brian attempted to create a unitary kingdom, calling himself *imperator Scottorum*, emperor of the Irish. The Battle of Clontarf, in April 1014, was cast in later Irish history as the successful culmination of his attempts to expel the hated Viking invader forever. It was, in fact, an example of how Irish and Viking politics had become intertwined: about half of the troops fighting for Sitric Silkenbeard, the Dublin king, were Leinster allies; Sitric himself was Brian's stepson and son-in-law, and was half-Irish; and far from wanting to extirpate Viking influence, Brian's ambition was to incorporate the bustling towns of Limerick, Waterford and Dublin into his 'empire'.

He had already taken Dublin once, on 1 January 1000, returning it to Viking control when Sitric submitted as his vassal. Dublin thrived under this arrangement, until Sitric joined a wider Irish revolt against Brian. Nor was the Clontarf battle itself decisive: Brian's forces did not manage to enter Dublin. Sitric (unlike Brian) survived and ruled Dublin until 1036. This is not to say that Clontarf was other than a highly significant event, one that was recalled for centuries throughout northern Europe; essentially it was a struggle for control of the lucrative Irish Sea trading network, with the powerful Orkney lord Sigurd the Stout taking the opportunity to muscle in on Dublin by supporting Sitric.

Ironically, the real effect of the battle was to prevent a non-Irish Viking takeover of Dublin. The way was open for Dublin to be more fully integrated into the rest of Ireland. This crozier, probably made in the town after the Battle of Clontarf, embodies the way the force that once terrified the monks had become part of the Irish world.

WHERE TO SEE IT: NATIONAL MUSEUM OF IRELAND-ARCHAEOLOGY, KILDARE STREET, DUBLIN 2; 00-353-1-6777444; WWW.MUSEUM.IE

This exquisite cross, which in the late-nineteenth century was in the possession of Fr Prendergast, the last abbot of Cong, Co. Mayo, was made c.1123, in Roscommon, probably for the diocescan centre of Tuam. The work is of the highest order: a core of oak, a large rock crystal, an elaborate mount and a flange decorated with gold filigree, niello (a deep-black mixture of metals) and blue and white glass studs. The cross chimes with other objects, such as the shrine of St Patrick's Bell, the high crosses of Kilfenora and Dysert O'Dea and the sarcophagus at Cormac's Chapel in Cashel, as expressions of a post-Viking Irish culture. All are heavily influenced by Hiberno-Norse design, in this case the so-called Urnes motifs (named after a site in Norway) of S-shaped animals interwoven with threadlike snakes.

The cross is a typically eclectic object. The head of the beast that grips the base has been compared to German Romanesque models. At the same time, this is a culmination of a long tradition of Irish ecclesiastical metalwork. Dr Pat Wallace, former director of the National Museum, has described it as 'both the last and one of the finest artistic efforts of our entire Early Christian period'. The cross's significance, however, goes beyond its artistic beauty. It can be seen as a weapon in the endless struggle for overlordship in Ireland. This is not just a crucifix for church worship; it is a shrine designed for the public display in procession of the most prestigious of mediaeval relics: an alleged fragment of the True Cross on which Christ was crucified, originally contained behind the central crystal. The Cross of Cong is 76cm high, but in procession it was held even higher on a staff or pole. It was meant to invoke awe.

The context for this is the vacuum in power that followed the Battle of Clontarf, which both curtailed the Vikings and ended the imperial ambitions of Brian Bóruma. The Irish annals mention cath Saxan, 'the Battle of the English'—the Norman invasion of 1066 that would have momentous consequences for Ireland—but these noises off did not distract from the internal struggles for dominance. The Cross of Cong was commissioned by the king of Connacht, Toirrdelbach Ua Conchobair (Turlough O'Connor), who was attempting to establish himself as high king of Ireland. He mounted successful campaigns against Munster and Dublin. His overlordship was never uncontested, but it acquired a crucial claim to legitimacy when he was given a fragment of the True Cross, which may have been brought to Ireland in 1123 as a means of encouraging (with limited success) Irish participation in Pope Calixtus II's crusade to the Holy Land. The Cross of Cong is thus a direct product of both international and Irish political machinations.

Not even the power of the True Cross, however, was enough to establish Toirrdelbach as a secure, centralised monarch of Ireland. Irish politics remained Byzantine and often bloody, with no one dynasty able to exert national control. This created a situation wide open to exploitation by opportunists already well entrenched across the Irish Sea.

WHERE TO SEE IT: NATIONAL MUSEUM OF IRELAND-ARCHAEOLOGY, KILDARE STREET, DUBLIN 2; 00-353-1-6777444; WWW.MUSEUM.IE

After the English king Harold Godwinson was defeated by the invading forces of William the Bastard, duke of Normandy, at the Battle of Hastings in 1066, his royal banner was taken to Dublin by his fleeing sons. It ended up in the hands of the high king, Toirrdelbach Ua Briain. The image of the Irish king flaunting the banner of a defeated English sovereign has a tragicomic irony.

There is little sense that Irish rulers in the decades after 1066 fully understood the implications of William's victory. The Normans were ruthless, thorough and efficient conquerors. Their origins were in the Viking terrorisation of France that had forced the Frankish monarchy to cede them control of what came to be called Normandy. In England, they mixed extreme violence with cold calculation. During the so-called Harrying of the North in 1069–70, the Normans destroyed food stocks to create a murderous famine. Yet their operation was mostly a classic case of what historians call 'elite transfer': 5,000 families took ownership of English estates without disturbing the underlying economic structures. This elite was emphatically military: the heavily armoured Norman knight, virtually fused with his huge armoured horse into a terrifying machine, was a product of great wealth and highly specialised training.

It was inevitable that, having consolidated their rule in England and subdued Scotland and Wales, they would look to Ireland. Successive attempts to establish an effective unitary Irish kingdom had failed; the annalists had a stock formula for the chief ruler: 'high king with opposition'. As early as 1155, at the Council of Winchester, the Anglo-Norman king Henry II discussed a possible invasion of Ireland. As it happened, internecine warfare allowed an opportunist lord, Richard de Clare, whom Henry had deprived of his title of earl of Pembroke, to beat the king to the punch.

In 1166, would-be high king Ruaidrí Ua Conchobair defeated and banished the Leinster overlord Diarmait Mac Murchada. Diarmait offered his allegiance to Henry II and received permission to recruit allies in Wales. In 1167 with the help of a small force of Flemings under Richard fitz Godebert, Diarmait reclaimed part of his kingdom. More Anglo-Norman adventurers arrived to support him, with Robert fitz Stephen, Hervey de Montmorency and Maurice de Prendergast helping him take Wexford. The most significant arrival was de Clare, known in Irish history by his nickname Strongbow. He captured Waterford in August 1170, married Diarmait's daughter Aífe, went on to take Dublin and fought alongside Diarmait until the latter's death, in 1171.

Strongbow summed up the qualities of the Anglo-Norman elite: energetic opportunism, military prowess and acquisitive efficiency. He died in Dublin in April 1176. The plain, almost blunt monument that stands over his grave in Christ Church is at best a symbolic representation of Strongbow. His original monument was, as an inscription recalls, 'broken by the fall of the roof' in 1562 and 'set up again'. Strongbow's most important monuments were to prove more enduring.

100 WHERE TO SEE IT: CHRIST CHURCH CATHEDRAL, CHRISTCHURCH PLACE, DUBLIN 8; 00-353-1-6778099; WWW.CHRISTCHURCHDUBLIN.IE

Laudabiliter satis et fructuose de glorioso nomine propagando in terres…tua magnificencia cogita: 'Quite laudably and profitably, your majesty considers how to extend the glorious name on earth…' Perhaps the most controversial object in Irish history is one that may not exist. *Laudabiliter*—the name of a bull issued by Pope Adrian IV to the English king Henry II in 1155—granted Henry the right to claim lordship over Ireland. Or did it? In the bull, Adrian (the only English pope) praises Henry's plan to 'reveal the truth of the Christian faith to peoples still untaught and barbarous and to root out the weeds of vice from the Lord's field'. He then permits Henry to enter Ireland in pursuit of these good causes and expresses the wish that 'the people of that land may receive you honourably and respect you as their lord'. The earliest source for the text of *Laudabiliter* is that seen here, in the *Expugnatio Hibernica* of the Cambro-Norman propagandist Giraldus Cambrensis.

Giraldus, the first foreigner to write a book on Ireland, came to Ireland at least three times (1183, 1185 and 1188) to see relatives among the Anglo-Norman invaders. He wrote his text to justify Henry's claims and to further his own career in the church. Henry did not refer to *Laudabiliter* when he landed near Waterford in 1171; it does not appear in the English or Vatican archives; it is not referred to in subsequent papal correspondence with Henry. Giraldus, moreover, was not averse to a spot of forgery: *Expugnatio* also contains a letter from Adrian's successor as pope, Alexander III, that few believe to be gen-

uine. It is almost certain that Adrian did write to Henry regarding Ireland, and Giraldus's text may even be partly genuine. As Professor Anne Duggan has pointed out, however, it fails to follow the format of every known papal declaration of the period. She suggests that Giraldus altered the order of the pope's paragraphs to make the bull read like a stronger endorsement of a putative conquest of Ireland than it actually was. Moreover, Giraldus omitted paragraphs that required Henry to seek the consent of Irish bishops and rulers for his overlordship.

Laudabiliter is a dodgy dossier. Henry's invasion of Ireland was pre-emptive. His fear was that Strongbow would establish himself as king of Leinster (through his marriage to Diarmait Mac Murchada's daughter Aífe) or even of Ireland. Henry's show of force (thousands of troops arrived with him in Waterford in October 1171) was aimed as much at his own Anglo-Norman vassals as it was at the native Irish. Henry's ships were loaded not just with arms but with sealing wax, the material needed for royal edicts, but also for authenticating charters by which he granted away entire Irish kingdoms. Irish kings and chieftains were quick to declare their loyalty. The submissions of Diarmait Mac Carthaigh of Desmond and Domhnall Mór Ua Briain of Thomond were followed, on Henry's progress northwards, by those of the kings of north Leinster, Bréifne, Airgialla and Ulster. The relative ease with which these rulers became subject to a distant Anglo-Norman king sharply contrasts with their unwillingness to submit to one of their own.

uit. Meilerio uo tanquam mar
chioni remotiore. proximu aut
Dublinie qui 7 olim stephani
de regia munificentia sibi ar
signat? fratrib; herefordensib;.

priuilegiu imperatio

Istea cm̃qm martiu plimu fre
c. 7 decenc exercitiu. anglop rex
sue tn̄ int agendu hybnie n̄ im
memor. cu prenotatis spurciciam
librciis 7 sinodo kassiliensi p indus
triam quesitis. directis ad curia
romanam nuntiis. ab adriano papa
de Anglia oriundo tũc presidente. priuilegiu im
petrauit. eidem auctoritate simt
7 ascensu. hybruco poplo tã do
minandi. eũ ipm in fidi rudi
mentis incultissimis. ecclastici
normis 7 disciplinis iuxt anglica
ne ecclie mores. 7 formandi. Iu
hybniam itaq priuilegio tũsmil
lo. p Nicholau Gualingefordensẽ
tunc priorem. malmesburiensẽ cm̃
priuodũ abbatẽ tã positũ cm̃ de
positũ. nec̃ 7 Guillelmum Alde
lim filium. conuocata stati apt
Guaerfordiam epop sinodo. in
publica audientia eidem priuile
giu 7 uniuersitatis assensu iosep
mi recitaũ facta fuit. Neon 7 al
cius priuilegii p eosdem cm̃similẽ
cp idem rex ab Adriano papa
Alex̃ decessore antea peruiserat.
p iohẽm salesburiensem. pniodc
epin karnotensem. romã ad hoc
destinatũ. p quem 7 idem papa

---

anglop regi anulum aureu. in
titure signum presentauit. Qui
stati simul cũ priuilegio 7 archiui
Guintonie repositus fiat. vn̄ re
iusdem priuilegii tenorem hic iserere
re. t̃ superfluu reputaui fiat icp
pm 7 pmo imperitati tenorẽ. Adri
anus eps seruus seruop dei kiño 7
xp̃o filio illustri anglop regi sa
lute. Et aplicam benedictõne. Lau
dabiliter 7 fructuose de glioso noie
ppagando in terris. 7 etne felicitatis
pmio cumulando in celis. tua mag
nificentia cogitat. Dum ad dilara
dos ecclie terminos. ad declaranda
indoctis 7 rudib; poplis xp̃iane fidi
ueritatem. 7 uitiop plantaria de ag
dominico extirpanda. sicut ca
tholic̃ pnceps intendis. ad id cõ
uenienti execuiendum. consiliũ
aplice sedis exigis 7 fauorẽ. Iu quo
facto cm̃to altiori consilio 7 maio
ri discretione pcedis. tanto 7 eo fel
ciorem progressum. te prestante dño
confidimus habiturū. eo cp̃ ad bon̄
exitum semp 7 finem soleant at
tinge. que de ardore fidi 7 religio
nis amore. principium acceperint.
Sane hybniam 7 oms insulas cp̃
bz sol iustitie xp̃e illuxit. 7 cp̃ docu
mita fidi xp̃iane ceprunt. ad i beati
ti petri 7 sacrofce romane ecclie.
cp̃ tua 7 nobilitas recognoscit. n̄
dubiũ ptinere. vn̄ tanto in eis li
bentius plantatõnem fidelem 7
gimen gtum deo inserim? cũ tõ co

47. FIGURE OF A HORSEMAN, THIRTEENTH CENTURY

It may not look much, but this damaged figure of a horse and rider, found in 1844 at Knockmannan Hill near Kinnitty, Co. Offaly, tells an important story. As a piece of freestanding sculpture of a nonreligious subject it is rare, but its significance lies in something that would have been immediately obvious to any thirteenth-century viewer; the horseman is Anglo-Norman. How do we know? He is using a humble object that made a big impact on European history: the stirrup.

Images of the Norman knight centre on the big-ticket items of military hardware: the armour, the kite-shaped shield, the lance, but what made the Norman cavalry charge so mighty a force was the humble stirrup, which anchored the rider to his horse and gave him the control necessary for disciplined concerted action. Irish cavalry, by contrast, were lightly armed and did not use stirrups. Nevertheless, these military advantages did not allow the Anglo-Normans to subdue Ireland easily. Henry II's power was threatened by revolts in his Breton and Gascon territories, drawing some of his followers away from Ireland.

Conflict with Irish kings continued. In 1175, Henry signed the Treaty of Windsor, witnessed by the archbishop of Dublin, Lorcán Ua Tuathail, assigning Dublin and the south-east to the Anglo-Normans and the rest of Ireland to the control of the high king, Ruaidrí Ua Conchobair. The deal, however, broke down—neither Henry nor Ruaidrí was able to exert authority over his own side. Rapacious Anglo-Norman warlords continued to carve out new territory, with John

de Courcy invading Ulster in 1177. Henry's appointment of his ten-year-old son, John, as Lord of Ireland that same year did nothing to end the turbulence. When John finally came to his Irish domain in 1185, his stay was brief and ineffective. Irish history might, nonetheless, have been different had John managed to establish a separate Irish kingdom. Instead, he succeeded his brother Richard as king of England in 1199, and Ireland remained as a 'lordship'.

Although fighting with Irish kings continued during John's reign, the Anglo-Norman colony did consolidate itself, literally, by placing those most imposing new features on the Irish landscapes— castles. Castles were not unknown in Ireland: Toirrdelbach Ua Conchobair built three in Connacht in 1124, but the scale of the castles John had built at Lismore, Dublin, Limerick and elsewhere, or those built by Hugh de Lacy along the north-east coast, was new. They gave imposing physical form to more subtle changes, such as the introduction of the first national coinage and of English common law.

Armed adventurers were followed by farmers, traders, clerics and administrators. These 'Normans' who came to Ireland did not necessarily have their roots in Normandy—many had English, Welsh, Flemish or Breton forebears. Indeed, the loss of Normandy itself to the English in 1204 spurred on the development of the colony in Ireland. During the thirteenth century, it created a system new to Ireland: that of villages, manors, parish churches and the most loved of Irish entities, the county.

WHERE TO SEE IT: NATIONAL MUSEUM OF IRELAND-ARCHAEOLOGY, KILDARE STREET, DUBLIN 2; 00-353-1-6777444; WWW.MUSEUM.IE

The Domhnach Airgid—or Silver Church—is a splendid exercise in mediaeval retro. It is not just an antique; it is a very deliberate display of self-conscious antiquity. One of the reasons the Anglo-Normans represented a far more potent threat to the established order in Ireland than the Vikings had ever done is that these newcomers were enormously interested in controlling the Irish church. The reform of a supposedly deca-dent Irish Christianity was a key ideological justification for the Anglo-Norman invasion. This also justified the supplanting of native by foreign abbots and bishops.

Long before the coming of the Anglo-Normans, however, the Irish church was in touch with the reforming movements of European Christianity. The reorganisation of the Irish church into territorial dioceses on the continental model was likewise undertaken before the Anglo-Norman invasion. The great continental monastic orders were already established in Ireland, notably at the Cistercian abbey of Mellifont, which had been founded in 1142 by monks from Clairvaux.

The newcomers nevertheless had a huge im-pact on the church in Ireland. They brought—in tandem with their establishment of lordly manors—the system of parishes that has had such a profound impact on the Irish sense of be-longing. They encouraged the rapid expansion of the Cistercians, Benedictines and Augustinians, as well as the introduction of new orders such as the Templars and Hospitallers. This influx created a di-rect challenge to the authority of native bishops, not least when, in 1217, it was decreed that, as 'the peace of Ireland has been frequently dis-turbed by elections of Irishmen' as bishops, none should be consecrated in future—a move de-nounced by the pope as an 'unheard of audacity'.

Part of the fightback by the native clerical aristocracy can be seen in a rash of elaborate re-furbishments of ancient sacred objects associated, especially, with the founder of the Irish church, St Patrick. The Domhnach Airgid was made to en-close a miscellany of relics. Traditionally, the shrine was claimed to be that given by St Patrick himself to his companion St Macartan, making it an ob-ject of great veneration.

Around 1350, the abbot of Clones, Co. Monaghan, John O Carbry, commissioned a substantial remodelling of the Domhnach Airgid. This remodelling brings the ancient relic up to date, in the international gothic style. It fuses contemporary feudal ideals with an insistence on the validity of indigenous traditions: native saints (Macartan, Patrick, Brigid, Columba) take their place alongside some late-mediaeval newcomers (Catherine of Alexandria, James the Great and John the Baptist in tandem with Salome). Already, an object from the distant Irish past is being used to make a contemporary political point.

WHERE TO SEE IT: NATIONAL MUSEUM OF IRELAND-ARCHAEOLOGY, KILDARE STREET, DUBLIN 2; 00-353-1-6777444; WWW.MUSEUM.IE

In the 100 years after the Anglo-Norman invasion, more new towns were established in Ireland than at any other period before or since. The existing Hiberno-Norse cities of Cork, Wexford and Limerick were rejuvenated, while Henry II declared Waterford and Dublin royal ports. The towns became centres of an increasingly efficient governing bureaucracy of mayors, judges and tax collectors.

Waterford, where both Strongbow and Henry had landed, initially enjoyed the biggest boost, becoming the main link between Ireland and the royal house of Anjou's rich possessions in France. In the early-thirteenth century, however, this pre-eminence was threatened by the rise of William Marshall, husband of Strongbow's daughter. Marshall, who developed his own port at New Ross, became immensely powerful, effectively ruling England as regent for three years after the death of King John in 1216. With the accession of Henry III, Waterford again pressed its claims to a monopoly on shipping. The result was a compromise: all ships, except those connected to Marshall's English or Irish possessions, would have to land at Waterford.

The compromise was unenforceable, and there were several pitched battles as Waterford tried to prevent ships landing at New Ross. Eventually, with the general decline in trade in the fourteenth century, Waterford's authorities took their claim for a renewed monopoly to King Edward III in 1373. They created a four-metre-long charter roll, containing documents or transcripts relating to the city going back to 1215. The charter roll also has seventeen remarkable illustrations. Among them are portraits of five kings of England, including the earliest contemporary portrait of a mediaeval English monarch, Edward III (shown opposite); the earliest portraits of a judge in either Britain or Ireland; of justiciars (governors of Ireland); of the mayors of Dublin, Waterford, Cork and Limerick; and the earliest view of an Irish city, Waterford itself.

Eamonn McEneaney of Waterford Museum of Treasures calls the charter roll 'the mediaeval equivalent of a PowerPoint presentation', designed to 'flatter the king, add weight to the legal arguments and keep those listening to the mayor's presentation focused on the facts being elaborated'. The roll is a brilliant early example of targeted advertising. It worked: the king restored Waterford's shipping monopoly.

The bitterness of the fight over commercial privileges between Waterford and New Ross shows that, even in the crisis-ridden fourteenth century, there was much to fight over. The variety of trade pursued in Anglo-Norman Ireland can be judged from the range of goods on which tolls were levied in the towns: wine, salt, foodstuffs, horses, cattle, hides, wool, cloth, iron, lead, tin, dyes, timber, millstones, nails, wax and so on. Town life was abuzz with small industry. The Great Parchment Book of Waterford (1361–1649) lists goldsmiths, tailors, shoemakers, weavers, mercers, cordwainers, tanners, saddlers, smiths, carpenters, masons, fishermen, vintners, butchers, bakers and millers. Most, to judge from their surnames, came from southwest England. Their descendants became a permanent part of Irish life.

IOI

WHERE TO SEE IT: **MEDIEVAL MUSEUM**, WATERFORD MUSEUM OF TREASURES, THE VIKING TRIANGLE, WATERFORD; 00-353-51-304500; WWW.WATERFORDTREASURES.COM

The significance of these coins is not the objects themselves, a penny from the 1280s (top) and a groat from 1460, but the gap of almost 200 years between them. Coins are tokens of the health of the colonial Anglo-Norman economy in Ireland. That the colony produced virtually no new coins for such an extensive period is striking evidence of the series of disasters that overtook it during the fourteenth century.

'When sorrows come', says Hamlet, 'they come not single spies, but in battalions'. Four big battalions of sorrows beset Anglo-Norman Ireland: the invasion of Edward Bruce from Scotland, the Great European famine, the Black Death and the Hundred Years War. The long and bloody wars of the fourteenth century, as the English monarchy struggled to assert control over France, took a heavy toll on the Irish colony, used as a source of men, provisions and money for the English war machine.

In 1315 the Scottish king (of largely Anglo-Norman stock) Robert Bruce was at war with England; he sent his brother Edward to Ireland to open a second front. Bruce was proclaimed King of Ireland by his Irish supporters on his arrival in 1315. His attack on Dublin was repulsed, however, and he was killed in 1318. His intervention was disastrously destructive: the Irish annals described him as 'the destroyer of Ireland in general'. Irish forces took advantage of the Bruce invasion to plunder Anglo-Norman towns, with the O'Tooles and O'Byrnes attacking the coastal towns of Wicklow, the O'Mores raiding Laois and the O'Hanlons besieging Dundalk.

Concentrated as it was in crowded and un-hygienic towns, the Anglo-Norman population was much more susceptible than the rural native populace to the ravages of epidemic disease. The Black Death, the combination of bubonic and pneumonic plague that decimated Europe, was preceded in Ireland by severe outbreaks of small-pox and influenza in 1327 and 1328. The plague arrived in 1348 and raged for three years. The Kilkenny friar John Clyn wrote of himself 'as if among the dead, waiting till death do come'. It has been estimated that the Black Death killed between one-quarter and one-third of the population, with disproportionate mortality again in the towns. Some medieval towns, such as Fore, in Co. Westmeath, and New Town Leys, in Co. Laois, disappeared altogether.

It has been estimated that Ireland's population had risen to over one million by 1300. By the fifteenth century it may have fallen to as few as 500,000. This decline affected the indigenous population as well as the colonisers, but the balance between them also shifted. The extent of Anglo-Norman control shrank, remaining strong in the areas around Dublin and east Leinster but becoming intermittent elsewhere. The revenue of the Irish exchequer declined and English monarchs were forced to contemplate new invasions to re-establish what had once seemed a secure lordship.

WHERE TO SEE THEM: NATIONAL MUSEUM OF IRELAND-DECORATIVE ARTS AND HISTORY, COLLINS BARRACKS, BENBURB STREET, DUBLIN 7; 00-353-1-6777444; WWW.MUSEUM.IE

Actual size.
Diam. 1.9cm

Actual size.
Diam. 2.5cm

What is most interesting about this cross is that it was given to the Franciscan friary at Lislaghtin, Co. Kerry, by Cornelius Ó Conchobhair and his wife, Avelina (Eileen), daughter of the Knight of Kerry. It marks a new prominence of high-status women in fifteenth-century Ireland. The cross, the finest of its kind from mediaeval Ireland, is of gilt silver. The elongated figure of the crucified Christ was surrounded by the symbols of the four evangelists; that for St Matthew, at the foot of the cross, is now missing. Figures of Franciscan friars decorate the base.

It is in late-mediaeval Ireland that high-status women begin to appear as patrons of monasteries and abbeys. The shrines of the *Book of Moling* and the *Stowe Missal* record the names of female as well as male patrons. The 1451 obituary of Margaret O'Carroll, daughter of Tadc O'Carroll, lord of part of what is now Tipperary, describes her death as a loss to 'all the Learned in Ireland', including 'both philosophers and poets'. It also has her 'preparing high-ways and erecting bridges, churches and Mass books', suggesting that she could deploy considerable financial and organisational resources. Margaret also took part in a large-scale Irish pilgrimage to the shrine of Santiago de Compostela in northern Spain.

There is some evidence of women being literate and formally educated in the late-fifteenth century, especially in the Anglo-Norman-controlled areas. Six monastic schools on crown lands are mentioned in 1539 as educating 'both gentilmen childer and other, both of man kynd and women kynd'. It is not clear how long these schools had been established, but their existence suggests that the new humanist idea of giving girls access to formal education had some purchase in Ireland. Within the colony, women could achieve significant status. Townswomen could trade and make contracts on their own behalf. Some Anglo-Irish women managed huge estates while their husbands were away, often for lengthy periods, on military service. Equally, the status of women of the landowning class was somewhat enhanced by provisions for inheritance under English (feudal) law. Under Irish (Brehon) law, women were not allowed to inherit collective property. Feudal law allowed a woman to inherit property if there was no male heir. This created in Ireland a degree of inheritance shopping, with rich families using whichever system suited their circumstances best.

Yet, for both the Irish and the Anglo-Irish, marriage seems to have been a moveable feast, and divorce was easily available. It remained normal for upper-class men and women to have a succession of spouses. Dubhchabhlaigh Mór ('the Great'), daughter of the king of Connacht, who died in 1395, was known as *Port-na-dtrí-namhad* ('Meeting place of the three enemies'), because she married in succession three sworn foes. It is interesting that when, after about 1400, the Irish adopted the common European practice of requiring a new wife to bring a dowry, it was with the proviso that the dowry must be returned in the event of a divorce.

One striking thing about the culture of fifteenth-century Ireland is what is not represented in it. There is not, to any great extent, evidence of that great flowering of European intellectual and artistic life that is summed up in the term Renaissance. The magnificent set of fifteenth-century Benediction copes and Mass vestments that survives from Christ Church cathedral in Waterford stands out as a rare example of Renaissance art in Ireland; but it could not be other than a European import.

The vestments are first mentioned in 1481 in the will of John Collyn, dean of the cathedral. They are likely to have been commissioned by a wealthy local patron and must have cost a fortune: the fabric is Italian cloth-of-gold and the embroidery is Flemish, probably from the great workshops of Brussels, Bruges or Ghent. When Oliver Cromwell's troops took the city in 1650 many of the city's great religious treasures were destroyed. The vestments, however, were so well hidden that they were not discovered again until 1774, when the old cathedral was demolished.

The most important part of the collection is the set of copes (liturgical mantles or cloaks): the red Creation Cope, illustrating the mystery of the Incarnation; the green Crucifixion Cope; a second green Marian Cope with marvellous velvet, and, featured here, the Magi Cope. It is staggeringly opulent: one-and-a-half metres high and two metres wide, brocaded velvet on cloth-of-gold, with a pile of red silk fixed with tiny loops of gold. The velvet almost certainly came from the Florence of Lorenzo Medici. The opulence is visual and metaphorical as well as physical. The hood of the Magi Cope alone depicts three parallel Biblical scenes: the homage of the Magi to the newborn Christ at the centre, the arrival of the Queen of Sheba at the court of King Solomon on the left and the visit of Abraham to Melchizedek on the right.

The Flemish artists who designed the Magi scene almost certainly drew on depictions in a book that typified the spread of learning in the Renaissance period that was made possible by printing: the *Biblia Pauperum*, the 'Bible of the Poor' that was hugely popular in Germany and the Netherlands. Thus, the cope brings together some of the forces that were shaping western European culture: the burgeoning wealth of the Italian city states, the spread of books, the skills of a growing artisan class, a new visual imagery that implies a new way of seeing the world. Nothing like this could have been made in fifteenth-century Ireland. The Renaissance was above all an urban phenomenon, and in Ireland at the time urban settlement was, if anything, being reversed. Ireland was never cut off from the great cultural awakening, but experienced it largely as an import.

WHERE TO SEE IT: **MEDIEVAL MUSEUM, WATERFORD MUSEUM OF TREASURES,** THE VIKING TRIANGLE, WATERFORD; 00-353-51-304500, WWW.WATERFORDTREASURES.COM

53. DE BURGO–O'MALLEY CHALICE, 1494

An inscription on this fine silver chalice, perhaps given to the Dominican abbey of Burrishoole, in Co. Mayo, in 1494, bears the names of Thomas de Burgo and his wife, Gráinne Ní Mháille (Gráinne O'Malley). The first surname is that of a scion of one of the great Anglo-Norman warlord families in Ireland; the second is obviously Gaelic. (Gráinne was an ancestor of the famous Granuaile.) The chalice—Michael Kenny of the National Museum of Ireland suspects it was probably made in Galway—is a physical token of the integration of the former invaders into Gaelic aristocratic society. Its Gothic style reveals a continuous exposure of Irish art to a shared European heritage.

The de Burgo presence in Ireland dates to the late-twelfth century, when William de Burgo was granted land in Tipperary by Lord John, the future King of England. William's son Richard invaded Connacht in the 1230s and, after a devastating series of conflicts, took control of most of it in 1235. The Bruce invasion and vicious infighting among various claimants to the de Burgo lordship gradually weakened it. Connacht was effectively lost to Anglo-Norman control, and hence to the English government, by 1350.

Anglo-Norman landholders—Burkes, Joyces, Stauntons—melted, as the chalice shows, into Gaelic upper-class society. In this sense, the chalice symbolises the revival of the Gaelic aristocracy and the retreat of the Anglo-Norman colony. The idea that Anglo-Norman Ireland was 'Gaelicised' in the fifteenth century neglects the fact that many of the major Anglo-Norman families resulted from marriages to high-status Irish women. For example, Thomas fitz Maurice, ancestor of the powerful Desmond clan, had an Irish wife called Sadhbh. The colonial aristocracy was always partly Irish, and the process of making it *Hiberniores Hibernis ipsis* (more Irish than the Irish) was a long one.

This process also involved more ordinary settlers. Hence, the Statute of Kilkenny, promulgated by Edward III's son Lionel, duke of Clarence, in 1366, complained 'many English…live and govern themselves by the manners, fashion and language of the Irish enemies'. Uniquely in the Christian world, the statute attempted to ban marriage between two Christian communities, the English and the Irish. Laws such as this were re-enforced by further parliamentary decrees even to the time this chalice was made, but the names inscribed on its base show how futile they were. Ironically, the English themselves began to think of the Anglo-Norman population of Ireland as simply Irish. In the fifteenth century, those of Anglo-Irish origin were officially classified in England as aliens. The earls of Desmond, descended from Thomas fitz Maurice, typified this new hybrid identity. Gerald FitzGerald was justiciar (royal governor) of Ireland in the 1360s but wrote Gaelic poetry. He had a daughter who did not know how to dress in English clothes and a son who was fostered by a Gaelic chief, Conor O'Brien of Thomond. It was increasingly necessary for such magnates to maintain theoretical loyalty to the English monarch while operating on the ground as Irish chieftains.

WHERE TO SEE IT: NATIONAL MUSEUM OF IRELAND-DECORATIVE ARTS AND HISTORY, COLLINS BARRACKS, BENBURB STREET, DUBLIN 7; 00-353-1-6777444; WWW.MUSEUM.IE

It is particularly ironic that the Gaelic kingship that best survived the Anglo-Norman invasion was that descended from Diarmait Mac Murchada, who had first brought Anglo-Norman warlords to Ireland. The Mac Murchadas retained lands in Carlow and north Wexford. The Kavanagh (Caomhánach) branch of the family, directly descended from Diarmait's son Domhnall Caomhánach, thrived as the Anglo-Norman colony weakened. Art Mór Mac Murchada had carved out a coherent kingdom by the time of his death, in 1416, successfully defying Richard II's attempts to have him removed.

This exotic object, preserved at Borris, Co. Carlow, by the Kavanagh family, perfectly captures this revival of Irish kingship. It is the only piece of Irish regalia to have survived from the mediaeval period. It was made from elephant ivory, sometime in the twelfth century, and may originally have been used as a hunting horn. In the period of Art Mór's resurgent kingdom it was given a new brass mounting—the maker's name, Tigernan O'Lavan, is inscribed on the mount—with clawed bird's feet on which it stands. This turned the horn into a ceremonial drinking vessel, probably for use in inauguration rituals. It was later used to further the Kavanaghs' claims to the kingship of Leinster.

That such a claim could be made at all was a remarkable historical reversal, given that Leinster had been so deeply penetrated and settled by the Anglo-Normans. By the 1420s, however, the area called the 'land of peace'—that is, under secure English administration—was confined to Dublin, Meath, Kildare and Louth. By the 1470s, this area was being referred to as the Pale. The revived Irish kingship outside that region was in many ways remarkably similar to what it had been before the Anglo-Norman invasion. The king was still drawn from a wide array of contenders, making civil wars of succession as common as they had been in the tenth century. The retinue of the king was also remarkably intact, with its hereditary ranks of brehons (judges), poets, genealogists, musicians and physicians. The expectation that a king could place his relatives in high clerical office was undiminished. Moreover, the economy on which this hierarchy rested was not all that different either. The land looked different in the places where the colonists had cleared the great forests. The tillage and grain-based agriculture introduced by the settlers retained a significant hold, but the revived Gaelic lordships still based their notions of wealth on cattle.

This strong element of cultural and economic conservatism is one of the factors behind the failure of these revived Irish kingships to cohere into anything like a national state. The resurgent Gaelic domains had little place for the urban life that was driving development in Europe. Even linguistic diversity was being rolled back: French disappeared in Ireland and English suffered a rare reversal. The Gaelic world that re-emerged never transformed itself into the kind of centralised, modernised political structure that could ultimately assert its independence.

WHERE TO SEE IT: NATIONAL MUSEUM OF IRELAND-ARCHAEOLOGY, KILDARE STREET, DUBLIN 2; 00-353-1-6777444; WWW.MUSEUM.IE

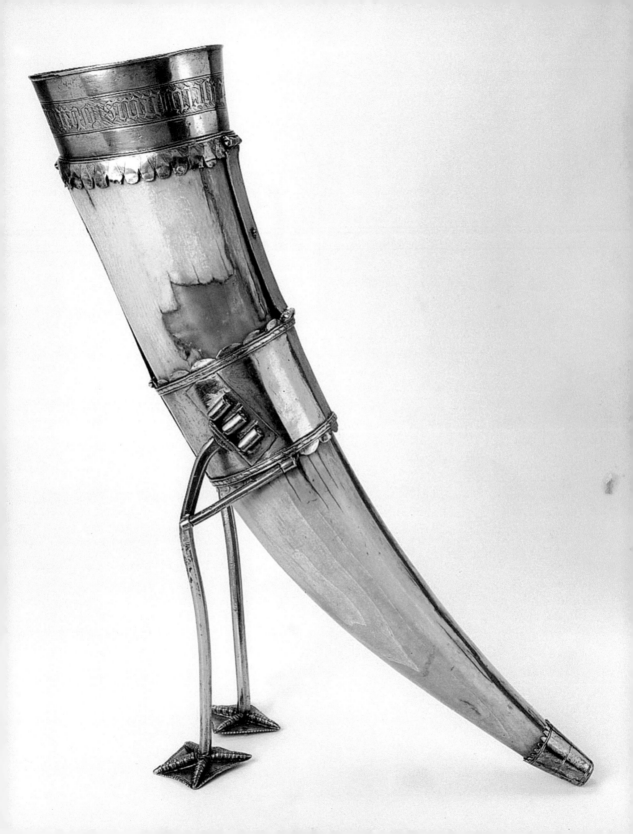

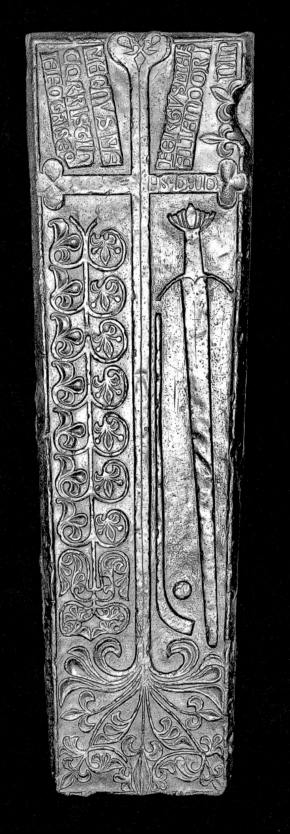

This 1.75 metre-long stone was uncovered in the graveyard of the ruined church at Clonca on the Inishowen peninsula, in Co. Donegal. Made of dark limestone, it is finely carved with a crucifix and a floral motif. The inscription says *FERGUS MAK ALLAN DO RINI IN CLACH SA/MAGNUS MEC ORRISTIN IA FO TRI SEO.* 'Fergus Mac Allan made this stone/Magnus Mac Orristin of the Isles under this covering'. Most striking are the images carved to the right of the cross: a sword and hurley and ball. The sword is a typical late-mediaeval variety from the west of Scotland. The hurley and ball suggest that Magnus was famed for his skill at what was called winter hurling, a form of the game played in the north of Ireland and in Scotland.

English sources divide Irish military forces into horsemen, kerns and gallowglasses. There were professional soldiers in the first two categories, but their ranks were swollen in times of war by ordinary farmers—only the clergy and the learned classes were exempted from duty. (Remarkably the Irish horsemen still refused to use stirrups —a striking testament to the conservatism of indigenous culture.) Gallowglasses, of whom Magnus was one, were professional soldiers. The word (*gallóglach*), which means 'foreign warrior', is first used in the late-thirteenth century in reference to mercenaries recruited from the mixed Scottish-Norse population of the Western Isles. Throughout the fourteenth century, large numbers continued to arrive from the islands and highlands of Scotland, drawn from the losing factions in internal conflicts.

From the beginning, however, these Gaelic-speaking mercenaries were integrated into Irish society. Two gallowglass families in particular became prominent in Irish affairs: the MacSweenys (former lords of Knapdale in Argyle) and the MacDonnells became, respectively, sub-chiefs of the O'Donnells and the O'Neills. The MacSweenys spread southwards from Tirconnell (Donegal) into Connacht and then into Munster, where they served the various MacCarthy clans. The MacDonnells, meanwhile, spread into Co. Mayo.

Gallowglasses had padded coats, helmets, daggers and the distinctive long-handled axes that marked them out. The warrior was accompanied by a manservant to carry his equipment and a boy to carry and cook his food; the unit of three was known as a spar, and 100 spars was the standard grouping. These men were quartered on the general population (a practice known as *bonnaght*), a cruel imposition in time of protracted war. As warriors, the gallowglass had a reputation for do-or-die courage. One account of 1534 notes that 'these sort of men be those that do not lightly abandon the field but bide the brunt to the death', and the annals mention whole battalions of gallowglasses dying together in battle. This professional ethic raised the level of militarisation in Gaelic society, making it a more formidable barrier to the expansion of English control.

113

 WHERE TO SEE IT: THE ORIGINAL IS IN CLONCA GRAVEYARD, INISHOWEN, CO. DONEGAL; THE CAST PICTURED IS IN THE GAA MUSEUM, CROKE PARK, ST JOSEPH'S AVENUE (OFF CLONLIFFE ROAD), DUBLIN 3; 00-353-1-8192323; WWW.CROKEPARK.IE/GAA-MUSEUM

This object is the first book printed in Ireland and, as such, marks the island's rather belated acquisition of one of the defining features of modernity. The revolutionary process of printing on a press with moveable type had been pioneered by Johannes Gutenberg in Germany almost exactly a century earlier. The delay in catching up with this new technology says much about Ireland's absence from the mainstream of the Renaissance, but if the advent of the first printed book brings a key aspect of modernity to Ireland, that modernity arrives in a form that is unwelcome to a substantial majority of the population.

Much of the initial impetus for the use of print was political and administrative, but it became an important weapon in the struggles between the energetic new Protestant faiths and the Catholic Counter-Reformation. The first uses of print in Ireland came in the wake of a failed rebellion against the crown by Silken Thomas FitzGerald, when the Tudor monarchy set about building an effective permanent government in Ireland. Printed royal orders were sent from London, as were printed copies of the submission to the crown of the powerful chieftain Con O'Neill. Print, therefore, arrived as an aspect of official power and propaganda.

Its effectiveness was limited in part by the limited knowledge of the English language in Ireland and in part by the absence of a resident printer. This latter problem was addressed in 1550 when the privy council granted £20 to establish Humphrey Powell, a London printer, in his trade in Dublin. His first task was to produce what the title page calls 'The boke of common praier and administration of the sacraments...after the vse of the churche of England'. That Church of England was, of course, itself a momentous development for Ireland. The product of Henry VIII's split from Roman Catholicism in the 1530s and the establishment of a national church headed by the monarch. The *Book of Common Prayer*, produced in 1549 under Henry's short-lived son Edward VI, was a major step towards the creation of an official and uniform Protestant religion. It was temporarily reversed under Edward's Catholic successor Mary, before being copperfastened under Elizabeth I.

The relative failure of the Protestant Reformation in Ireland is one of the great shaping forces of modern Irish history. Who knows how the island would have developed had the *Book of Common Prayer* eventually become as common and comfortable a presence in the average Irish home as it was in England? That this did not happen made Ireland one of the great exceptions to the compromise formula adopted throughout most of Europe after ferocious religious conflict: *cuius regio, eius religio*: the religion of the ruler will be the religion of his subjects. In Ireland a majority of those from both Gaelic and Anglo-Norman stock remained Catholic.

 WHERE TO SEE IT: LIBRARY OF THE ROYAL IRISH ACADEMY, 19 DAWSON STREET, DUBLIN 2; 00-353-1-6090620; WWW.RIA.IE/LIBRARY. GROUP VIEWING ONLY (BY APPOINTMENT). IMAGES FROM IMPERFECT RIA COPY; VIEW A MORE COMPLETE COPY IN TCD LIBRARY DIGITAL COLLECTIONS: HTTP://DIGITALCOLLECTIONS.TCD.IE/HOME/

O lambe of God that takeſt awaie the ſynnes of the woꝛlde:
>Haue mercie vpon vs.

O Chꝛiſt heare vs.
>O Chꝛiſt heare vs.

Loꝛde haue mercie vpon vs.
>Loꝛde haue mercie vpon vs.

Chꝛiſt haue mercie vpon vs.
>Chꝛiſt haue mercie vpon vs.

Loꝛde haue mercie vpon vs.
>Loꝛde haue mercie vpon vs.

Our father whiche arte in heauen. *with the reſidue of the pater noſter.*

And leade vs not into temptacion.
>But deliuer vs from euill.   Amen.
>The verſicle.

O Loꝛde deale not with vs after our ſinnes.
>Aunſwere.
>Neither rewarde vs after our iniquities.

>Let vs pꝛaie.

O God mercifull father, that deſpyſeſt not the ſighyng of a contrite hert, noꝛ the deſire of ſuche as be ſoꝛowfull, mercifully aſſiſt our pꝛaiers, that we make befoꝛe thee in all our troubles and aduerſities, when ſo euer thei oppꝛeſſe vs: And graciouſly heare vs, that thoſe euilles, whiche the crafte and ſubtiltie of the deuill oꝛ man woꝛketh againſt vs, be bꝛought to naught, and by the pꝛouidence of thy goodneſſe, they maie be diſperſed, that we thy ſeruauntes, beyng hurt by no perſecucions, maie euer moꝛe geue thankes vnto thee, in thy holy Churche, through Ieſu Chꝛiſt our Loꝛde.
>O Loꝛde, ariſe, helpe vs, and deliuer vs foꝛ thy names ſake.

O God we haue heard with our eares, and our fathers haue declared vnto vs, the noble wooꝛkes that thou bidſt in theyꝛ daies, and in the olde tyme befoꝛe theim.
>O Loꝛde, ariſe, helpe vs, and deliuer vs, foꝛ thy honour.

Gloꝛie be to the father. ⁊c.   As it was in the begin. ⁊c.

From our enemies defende vs, O Chꝛiſt.
>Graciouſely looke vpon our afflictions.

Pitifully behold the ſoꝛowes of our hert.
>Mercifully foꝛgeue the ſinnes of thy people.

Fauourablie with mercie heare our pꝛaiers.
>O ſonne of Dauid, haue mercie vpon vs.

Bothe now and euer voucheſafe to heare vs Chꝛiſt.
>Graciouſely heare vs, O Chꝛiſt.
>Graciouſely heare vs, O Loꝛde Chꝛiſt.

This incongruously elegant jewelled pendant was recovered from the wreck site of the Spanish galleass *La Girona*, which sank off Lacada Point, on the north Antrim coast, in the autumn of 1588. *Girona* was part of the largest invasion fleet yet assembled, the great armada of 130 ships that set sail from Lisbon on 30 May 1588. Its aim, as part of Philip II's crusade against Protestant 'heretics', was to depose Elizabeth I and presumably to re-establish a Catholic monarchy. (Philip had been married to Elizabeth's sister and predecessor, Mary.) Spain and England were already fighting a proxy war in the Low Countries; Philip was now intent on a comprehensive victory. On board the ships was a vast store of ordnance, including the massive siege guns intended to batter down the walls of London.

The pendant embodies the imperial power and commercial reach of Spain. Its body is of gold probably from the Spanish colonies in the new world of America. The rubies that marked out its spine and tail—three of the original nine survive—may have come from southern Asia. The fine workmanship in the detail of the scales, claws and tail adds to the flair of the object. The salamander is a real lizard but is also a mythical creature with the magical ability to survive and extinguish fire. For the officer who wore the pendant, it thus served as a talismanic protection against the danger of fighting on a wooden ship.

The charm was even more necessary than its owner must have hoped when *Girona* set sail. The armada was held up by English manoeuvres and unfavourable winds in the English Channel, and left with little choice but to try to return to Spain. Its commander, Medina Sidonia, warned his captains to 'take heed lest you fall upon the Island of Ireland for fear of the harm that may happen to you upon that coast'. The foul Atlantic weather took its toll: *Girona* was one of at least 26 ships that foundered off Ireland.

On board was a crew of 600; *Girona* rescued 700 more from other armada vessels that foundered. Among those who drowned were the captain, Fabricio Spinola, and one of the fleet's senior commanders, Alonso de Leiva. Most casualties were, as always, the anonymous foot soldiers of imperial wars. Just six are thought to have survived from *La Girona*. For those who did make it ashore, the land proved no safer than the sea. The English lord deputy, Fitzwilliam, gave instructions to 'apprehend and execute all Spaniards'.

In all about 5,000 Spaniards were drowned or killed, many by Irish lords who were fearful either of the Spaniards themselves or of the government. However, some of the nobles were captured and subsequently ransomed while others, notably Captain Francisco de Cuéllar, were given sanctuary by Irish lords until they could be spirited back to Spain. The wreckage of ships of the armada and the shore landings of Spaniards is called to memory by place names such as Carraig-na-Spania and Port na Spaniagh. Nevertheless, the failure of the armada, and the consequent consolidation of the Protestant monarchy of England, had enormous consequences for Ireland.

 WHERE TO SEE IT: NATIONAL MUSEUMS NORTHERN IRELAND-ULSTER MUSEUM, BOTANIC GARDENS, BELFAST BT9 5AB; 00-44-845-6080000; WWW.NMNI.COM/UM

The exact provenance of this morion—a helmet without a protective visor or beaver—is not clear. It was almost certainly made in Italy around 1580, and it reached Ireland as a result of efforts by the papacy or Spain to support Catholic rebellions. The disastrous landing at Ard na Caithne, or Smerwick, in Co. Kerry, that year, when mercenary troops funded by the papacy were executed after they had surrendered, was a prelude to a much more profound challenge to Tudor rule in Ireland. The Nine Years War of 1594 to 1603 was, for both sides, an existential struggle. The galvanising figure on the Irish side was Hugh O'Neill, second earl of Tyrone and, after 1595, a proclaimed traitor. Raised in English manners in the Pale, he later modernised the methods of raising, equipping and funding an Ulster fighting force, which he trained to stand firm and fight in an open field. He also fused religion and politics into a powerful ideology.

Previous Irish rebellions had appealed to a broad antipathy to England and Protestantism. In 1579, James Fitzmaurice Fitzgerald returned from continental military service bearing a papal indulgence for his followers and declaring a holy war against Elizabeth I, who had been excommunicated seven years previously. O'Neill, however, brought the idea of a specifically Catholic revolt to its fullest expression. The alliance he sought was for 'Christ's Catholic religion'. As the prospects of military aid from Spain grew brighter, he adopted the language of a struggle for 'the extirpation of heresy'. He gradually fused this religious war with an appeal for the 'defence of the native soil'. O'Neill translated this embryonic Catholic nationalism into a political manifesto, envisaging an early version of home rule whereby the English could appoint a viceroy but all civil posts would be held by Irishmen.

This political strategy was backed up with military muscle. O'Neill and his allies inflicted significant defeats on government forces notably at Clontibret, followed up with a stunning victory at the Yellow Ford in August 1598, smashing an army of 5,000 men under Sir Henry Bagenal. Despite these successes, O'Neill's revolt was weakened by his failure to seduce or bully the Old English of the towns. Diplomatically, he was limited by the unwillingness of Pope Clement VIII to declare his cause to be a crusade.

These problems meant that ultimate victory depended on support from Spain. It came on 21 September 1601, when 3,300 troops landed at Kinsale—far from O'Neill's Ulster stronghold and a dreadful site on which to withstand a siege. The English lord deputy, Charles Blount, Lord Mountjoy, locked the Spanish into Kinsale, forcing O'Neill and his ally Hugh O'Donnell to undertake a long march south to relieve them. When battle was finally joined, on 3 January 1602, it lasted just two hours but delivered a blow from which the Gaelic aristocracy would never recover. Kinsale was an epic disaster. O'Donnell left for Spain and died within months; O'Neill retreated to Ulster and fought on for another fifteen months, but something had ended, and it was not just a war.

118

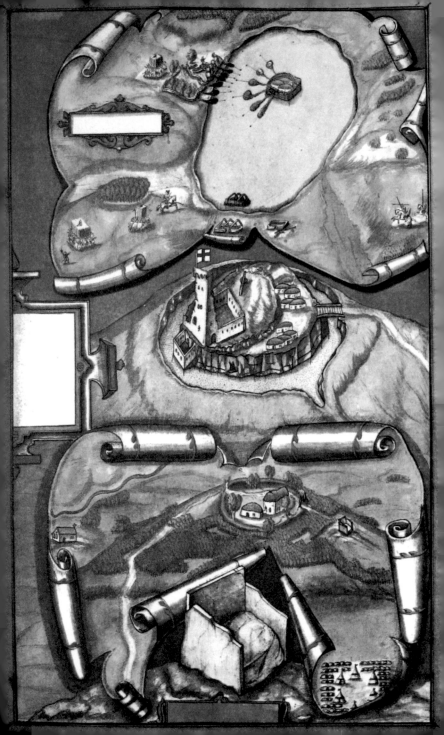

One of the most poignant objects in Irish history is one that was deliberately and symbolically destroyed. The partly wooded hill of Tulach Óg (Tullaghogue), north of Dungannon in Co. Tyrone, commanding extensive views towards Slieve Gallion, was one of many traditional ritual sites on which communities gathered and kings were inaugurated. The Tudor colonisers looked on these sites with suspicion. The poet Edmund Spenser called them the resort of 'all the scum of loose people'. The Tudors well understood the significance of Tulach Óg as the inauguration site for the O'Neill chieftains. The cartographers Francis Jobson and Richard Bartlett marked it prominently on their maps of Ulster—Bartlett's illustration is seen here.

The focal point of the site was a rough-hewn stone chair called *leac na ríogh* 'the flagstone of the kings', which is first recorded in the annals in 1432. From Bartlett's surviving drawing, it seems to have been made up of four pieces: a rough base (which may be the original stone) to which a back and sides were later added. This original stone may in turn have come from a part of the hill that was sacred as an ancient place of assembly. Archaeologist Elizabeth FitzPatrick suggests it may have been 'adopted by Cenél nÉogain'—the ancestors of the early mediaeval Uí Néill—'when they annexed the kingdom of Airgialla and established their new royal inauguration site at Tulach Óg in the tenth century'.

The stone, indeed, probably represented a tradition that went back to the pre-Christian past. Its rough form, barely transformed from its natural state, was deliberate. The king, at inauguration, was wedded to the goddess of sovereignty, representing the land from which the stone was drawn. The rough, almost natural shape was meant to convey something ancient and primal.

Leac na ríogh played an important symbolic role in Hugh O'Neill's rebellion against the Tudors and his establishment of himself as a Gaelic chieftain. Sir Henry Bagenal noted in 1595 that:

> Old O'Neyle is dead and the Traitour gone to the stone to receave that name.

At the beginning of September 1602, nine months after the Battle of Kinsale, Lord Deputy Mountjoy arrived at Tulach Óg while he was harrying Tyrone. He:

> spoiled the corn of all the country…and brake down the chair wherin the O'Neals were wont to be created, being of stone planted in the open field.

The pieces of the *leac* were said to be kept in the orchard of the glebe house of the local Protestant church until 1776, when the last of them was taken away.

There was an ironic coda. O'Neill's daughter Sorcha married a Magennis, one of whose descendants was Lady Glamis. In 1900, she had a daughter, Elizabeth Bowes-Lyon. Her daughter, in turn, is the current occupant of the British throne.

 WHERE TO SEE IT: SITE OF *LEAC NA RÍOGH* IS AT TULLAGHOGUE FORT, TULLYWIGGAN ROAD, TULLAHOGUE, COOKSTOWN, CO. TYRONE; 00-44-48- 8676 9949; WWW.DISCOVERNORTHERNIRELAND.COM/TULLAGHOGE-FORT-COOKSTOWN-P2950. BARTLETT MAP: NATIONAL LIBRARY OF IRELAND, KILDARE STREET, DUBLIN 2; 00-353-1-6030200; WWW.NLI.IE

What could be more English than a good wassail? From the Anglo-Saxon 'wael hael'—good health—the word refers to the tradition of ceremonial drinking of cider that survived strongly in south-west England.

In 1599 Arthur Chichester brought this wassail bowl from his native Devon to Ulster. It can be seen as a token of the idea that took shape in the plantation of Ulster: making Ulster British. Chichester was a classic Elizabethan adventurer. During the Nine Years War he was in command in north-east Ulster; led an amphibious assault across Lough Neagh into central Ulster; and obviously kept his eye open for good land in south Antrim, which he was duly granted after victory had been achieved. In 1608, he used his position as Lord Deputy to claim and acquire the entire Inishowen peninsula; in the Ulster plantation, he acquired an estate that included Dungannon, thus symbolically occupying what had been Hugh O'Neill's base of operations.

At first the attitude of the English government to the defeated Gaelic lords was conciliatory. The hope was that, suitably tamed, the Ulster aristocrats would settle down to administering the region for the crown. The Flight of the Earls marked the collapse of this policy. A bold new strategy began to take shape, partly at Chichester's prompting: if the population could not be coerced or cajoled into loyalty, change the population, as the crown had attempted to do in Munster after the defeat of the earl of Desmond.

Even before the Irish lords left land speculators had begun colonising east Ulster, but the process was accelerated by the confiscation of the land of the departed earls. A failed rising by Sir Cahir O'Doherty in Derry allowed the state to seize his lands too. Thus, six of the nine counties of Ulster—Armagh, Cavan, Coleraine (Derry), Donegal, Fermanagh and Tyrone—were crown possessions. In 1610, as sanctioned by James I, 40 per cent of this land was allocated to English or Scots 'undertakers', with the rest allotted to soldiers who had fought in the Irish campaigns, loyal Irish chieftains, the Church of Ireland and government officials. Undertakers were obliged to replace native Irish with settlers within two years and to build a castle on their lands by 1613. The creation of urban settlements was a key part of the 'civilising' project. Derry, renamed Londonderry, was treated separately and assigned to the City of London.

The plantation did not go to plan. Many undertakers lacked the capital to create and sustain large-scale settlements. In 1610 Chichester wrote that 'those from England are, for the most part, plain country gentlemen...If they have any money, they keep it close'. By 1630 the number of Scots in Ulster may have been as few as 16,000, with an even smaller number of English settlers. Undertakers had little choice but to keep on indigenous Catholics as tenants. This meant that there was less immediate social conflict than might have been expected. It also meant that Ulster evolved not as a model Protestant colony but as a much more complex and mixed society.

WHERE TO SEE IT: NATIONAL MUSEUMS NORTHERN IRELAND-ULSTER MUSEUM, BOTANIC GARDENS, BELFAST BT9 5AB, 00-44-845-6080000; WWW.NMNI.COM/UM

To the hon.ble y.e kn.te Cittizens & Burgesses in y.e Comons house of a Parliament
assembled in the Kingdome of England

The severall undernam.d dispoiled & distressed, Ladyes & Gentlewomen now
residing within y.e Citty of Dublin, & others in the kingdome of Jreland,
Jn humble manner represent theire miserable Condition

Sheweing, that y.o your supp.lients some have by gods great mercy & goodnes with y.e great hazard of theire
Lives by y.e other losses of their whole estates, escaped the fury of y.e Jrish rebells, whose unparalleld & cruilty
exercised on such as fell within theire power, doth sufficiently appeare

Some of them although resident in & about y.e Citty of Dublin yett had their estats lying furthest of
in y.e countrey possessed by the rebells

The wholly livelyhood also of others consisting in certaine somes of money, being y.e legacies left unto
them by theire deceased parents, all being either in the hands of such as now are in actuall rebellion or some
others as were by y.e rebells slaine or wholly stripped out of all, and therefore disenabled to answeare the necessities
of y.e supp.lients

By all w.ch y.e peticoners are distitute of all meanes of reliefe and now readie to perish, some of
them being reduced to such extremities that the selling away of their ordinary attire, & necessary wearing
apparell at great undervalues is the greatest part of theire present supply

And whereas of y.e peticoners many are of her condition, & others of the better ranke of
gentlewomen whereby they are uncapable of y.e ordinary provision already by y.e charitable & pious care
designed for y.e other poore of the inferiour sort, and therein yo.r supp.lients distitute, & laid open to apparant
ruine if not taken into yo.r consideracion

May it therefore please yo.r hono.rs among others yo.r Acts of charity to comiserate the
most distressed condicion of yo.r peticoners in thinking on such wayes & meanes for theire present sustinance
& subsistance as in yo.r wisdomes shalbe thought fitting

That by adding hereof to yo.r other great workes of pietie, you may
also add unto y.e list & oblige to bee in y.r numbers of yo.r daily
oratoryes, vo whose names are here subscribed

Anne Dowra

Anne Dowra   Mary Leigh   Anne Blayney

Eliza: Dowra   Kath Edgworth   Jane moore

Ma: Wyloughby   Allice Moore   Elizabeth Royce

Martha Ardine   Marie Blayney

Rebecka Hewetson   Alce Hammilton

Rebecka Hewetson fil.   Mary Butler

Mari Beare   Elyza: wizzall

Dorothy Moigne

Mary Arundell

Alce hamilton

valentine Hamilton

Judeth Allen

61. DEPOSITION ON ATROCITIES, 1641

Some objects resonate with their own times, but a few intrude themselves again and again into contemporary affairs. They remain available for use, not just as evidence of the past, but as warnings of a potential future. The 1641 Depositions—eight volumes of written testimonies of witnesses to the violent ethnic revolt that began in Ulster in that year and spread through much of the island, are objects of this sort. They contain evidence—mostly, but not exclusively, from Protestants—of murder, assault and theft. Right up to the twentieth century, they were deployed as proof of Catholic barbarism and malice, justifying everything from the campaigns of Oliver Cromwell to resistance to Home Rule.

Pamphlets and books such as James Cranford's *The Teares of Ireland* (1642), illustrated with luridly violent woodcuts, were circulated widely in England, along with hugely exaggerated claims for the numbers of dead. The depositions were taken, as the lords justices in London explained, because they might be of 'great use… hereafter in due time, both for His Majesty's advantage and perhaps the relief of some of the persons injured'. Many of the more sensational incidents were reported in hearsay. Phrases such as 'believeth', 'thinketh' and 'hath credibly heard' appear far more frequently in the deposition texts than 'saw' or 'witnessed'. Yet, there is no doubt that the depositions do contain real evidence of great cruelty and traumatic suffering.

Many Protestants were killed and many others died as a result of exposure to a bitter winter, or of famine, as they were driven from their homes. The burning of bibles and the stripping naked of victims had overtones of ritual humiliation and sectarian hatred. Catholics also died as a result of the chaos and upheaval: roughly 5,000 Catholics and the same number of Protestants perished in the winter of 1641–2. The rising was not merely a response to the plantation of Ulster: many of its Catholic leaders had, in fact, retained their own lands. The immediate context, rather, was British. Scottish Presbyterians had revolted against Charles I, who was also in deep dispute with his own parliament. The rising was thus initially aimed at exploiting the weakness of the monarchy to gain concessions for Catholics. Instead, it helped push both islands into civil war.

Rebel plans to seize Dublin Castle failed, but Sir Phelim O'Neill, nephew of Hugh O'Neill, occupied strongholds across south Ulster, beginning with Dungannon on 22 October 1641. He issued a proclamation ordering that no harm be done to English or Scots settlers and claiming that the rebels were looking merely for their own freedom. The government blamed 'ill-affected papists' for the rising, and indiscriminate sectarian retaliation against Catholics prompted the Old English Catholics to join forces with the rebels. A meeting near Trim, Co. Meath, in November sealed the alliance that became known as the Confederate Association.

The rising had enormous consequences, not just for Irish but also for British history. It fatally undermined Charles in his struggle with parliament, and it led, ultimately, to the very thing it was intended to forestall: a much greater expropriation of Catholic land and a triumph of Protestant power.

This superb silver chalice declares its origins very clearly. The engraving in Latin on the base reads: 'Malachy O'Queely Doctor of Sacred Theology from Paris and Archbishop of Tuam had this chalice made for the convent of friars minor of Rosserilly [Co. Galway], 1640'. O'Queely, with his continental connections, illustrates the key role played by the Franciscans in re-creating an Irish Catholic identity after the Flight of the Earls. The order established the Irish colleges at Louvain and Rome and revived their own houses in Ireland. The friars at Rosserrilly were expelled twice in the early-seventeenth century, but their presence was recorded in 1641, and the chalice possibly marks their return.

With its inscription 'I will lift up the cup of salvation and call on the name of the Lord', and its bold engravings of the Crucifixion alongside O'Queely's own coat of arms, the chalice speaks of a resurgent and militant faith. With the outbreak of a Catholic rebellion the year after it was made, O'Queely himself took up arms in its cause. After initial rebel successes in Ulster, the rebellion spread throughout the country. The indigenous and Old English sides of the Catholic elite formalised their alliance as the Confederate Association, with its capital in Kilkenny and its military organisation strengthened by the return from continental wars of veteran soldiers, most notably Owen Roe O'Neill. It was ostentatiously Catholic— its banners bore images of the Virgin Mary.

By the summer of 1642 the rebellion was close to collapse, but in August civil war broke out between King Charles I and his parliament in England. The resulting bloody stalemate of affairs in Ireland ended with the arrival in October 1645 of the papal nuncio, Archbishop Rinuccini, who became a strong voice of the Catholic leadership. In ethnically and religiously complex Ireland, three armed forces—royalist, confederate and Scots (the latter sent by Covenanters to protect Protestant settlers in Ulster)—became four in 1644, when the royalist commander in Munster, Lord Inchiquin, defected to the parliamentarian side.

In October 1645 O'Queely led his forces in an attempt to retake the port of Sligo, which had fallen to the parliamentarians. He was killed in a surprise attack and his army routed. A similar fate met confederate troops in 1647 when the Earl of Ormond surrendered Dublin to the parliamentarians, under Michael Jones. The latter then routed a large confederate army at Dungan's Hill outside the city. Large numbers of prisoners were put to the sword. In 1648 a second civil war erupted in England; the parliamentarian victory led to the execution of King Charles a year later. In Ireland, Jones's parliamentarian army repulsed Ormond's attack on Dublin, defeating his royalist forces at Rathmines, and clearing the way for the landing, in August 1649, of the triumphant New Model Army, led by Oliver Cromwell.

100 WHERE TO SEE IT: NATIONAL MUSEUM OF IRELAND-DECORATIVE ARTS AND HISTORY, COLLINS BARRACKS, BENBURB STREET, DUBLIN 7; 00-353-1-6777444; WWW.MUSEUM.IE

Oliver Cromwell's reputation in Ireland is bloody and bitter. That his one personal legacy to the country should be not only particularly beautiful but also rather erotic is history's little black joke. This very fine ebony cabinet is thought to have been made in Flanders, most likely Antwerp, around 1652. Antwerp became the leading European centre for painted cabinets, many of which were given as wedding gifts.

There is a tradition that Cromwell gave this one to his daughter Bridget when she married the lord deputy of Ireland, General Charles Fleetwood. (Bridget had previously been married to one of Cromwell's most feared generals, Henry Ireton, who died near Limerick in 1651.) If so, it was a lavish gift. Inlaid in the cabinet are ten painted scenes illustrating the erotic tales of the Roman poet Ovid, including Perseus rescuing Andromeda, the Rape of Europa and Venus being carried off by Jupiter in the form of a bull.

When Cromwell arrived in Ireland in August 1649, he was effectively the head of a republic. Victory over the forces of the Scottish Covenanters and of King Charles I had been followed by the latter's execution in January 1649. What remained to be achieved was the punishment and suppression of the Irish Catholic rebels, whom Cromwell saw as the perpetrators of barbaric massacres in 1641, and the mopping up of royalist resistance under the duke of Ormond. Ormond and the Catholic confederates, having fought each other for years, joined forces to oppose him.

Cromwell had a splendid, battle-hardened army of 12,000 men. Their republican ideology was not necessarily anathema to ordinary Irish people. The royalist commander in Wexford had trouble stopping locals from dealing with Cromwell's troops, as 'the rogues allure them by speaking that they are for the liberty of the commoners'. Cromwell himself had little interest in persuasion or conciliation. He made for Drogheda, which was garrisoned by royalist forces. After a siege, his troops massacred about 3,000 defenders, including many civilians. Cromwell made it clear that revenge for 1641 was on his mind: 'This is a righteous judgement of God upon these barbarous wretches, who have imbrued their hands in so much innocent blood'. (Many of those who died in his assault on Drogheda were English royalists or Irish Protestants.) In October, Cromwell repeated the lesson, massacring about 2,000 people in Wexford.

His subsequent campaigning was more moderate. He observed the terms of surrender at Clonmel in 1650, even though his army had been badly mauled in attacking it. Cromwell departed Ireland shortly after taking Clonmel, leaving the command to Ireton. The cost to Ireland as a whole was catastrophic: about 20 per cent of the population died from violence, famine and disease between 1649 and 1653. An account published in London in 1652 said, 'You may ride 20 miles and scarce discern any thing or fix your eye upon any object, but dead men hanging on trees and gibbets'.

100 WHERE TO SEE IT: NATIONAL MUSEUM OF IRELAND-DECORATIVE ARTS AND HISTORY, COLLINS BARRACKS, BENBURB STREET, DUBLIN 7; 00-353-1-6777444; WWW.MUSEUM.IE

64. BOOKS OF SURVEY AND DISTRIBUTION, MID-SEVENTEENTH CENTURY

There are very few plainer objects in this selection, but none that is more consequential. The so-called Books of Survey and Distribution, compiled between the 1650s and 1680s, record in micro-cosm the seismic shift in the ownership of land in Ireland after the Cromwellian conquest. The class of Catholic proprietors, of both indigenous and Anglo-Norman descent, was all but swept away.

These pages, from Book 17, show what hap-pened in just one parish: Kilcaruan in Duleek, Co. Meath. On the left-hand page are the names of the owners of lands in 1641, when the great Catholic uprising broke out. On the right-hand page are the names of those to whom the land was given after it had been expropriated. Accompanying the pages is the hand-drawn map of Meath from the Down Survey, which was used to record the major land holdings throughout Ireland so that the project of expropriation could be conducted properly.

Thus, we can see that most of the land in Kilcaruan was held in 1641 by what would then have been called Old English families—descen-dants of much earlier post-Norman settlers: Plunkett, Luttrell, Moore, Talbot, Allen. After 1641 these ethnic distinctions have been sunk in the crude code written after their names in the book: 'Ir. Pa.'—Irish papist. That in itself justifies the transfer of their lands to Protestant owner-ship—overwhelmingly to the earl of Anglesey. In each case the number of acres held in 1641 is the same as the number transferred—the expropria-tion was wholesale.

After the defeat of the Catholic rebellion, the Commonwealth administration undertook an ex-traordinarily ambitious programme of social engineering. Under the guise of the punishment of traitors, about half of all land in Ireland was taken from its owners and given to adventurers who had funded Cromwell's armies or to those who had served in his campaigns. The policy was modified but continued after the collapse of the Commonwealth and the restoration of the monar-chy. The scale of change was remarkable: the amount of land in Protestant hands went from 41 per cent of the total to 78 per cent in just 20 years.

It is not surprising that the names on the left-hand page feature heavily on the Jacobite side of the wars of the 1680s. A later Simon Luttrell, for example, was a prominent Jacobite cavalry com-mander and afterwards a colonel in the service of the Spanish monarchy. The new owner of the lands in Kilcaruan, on the other hand, was himself Irish. The earl of Anglesey was born plain Arthur Annesley on Fishamble Street in Dublin; his father was secretary of state for Ireland under Cromwell's son Henry. Arthur supported the par-liamentary side during the civil war, but he then became a key figure in the restoration of the monarchy under Charles II, being rewarded with an earldom and the lucrative position of vice treasurer and receiver general of Ireland from 1660 to 1667. He embodies, indeed, the great irony of the seventeenth-century land settlement: it was initiated by rebels against the crown but created a loyalist ruling class.

WHERE TO SEE IT: NATIONAL ARCHIVES OF IRELAND, BISHOP STREET, DUBLIN 8; 00-353-1-4072300 OR 1890-252424; WWW.NATIONALARCHIVES.IE

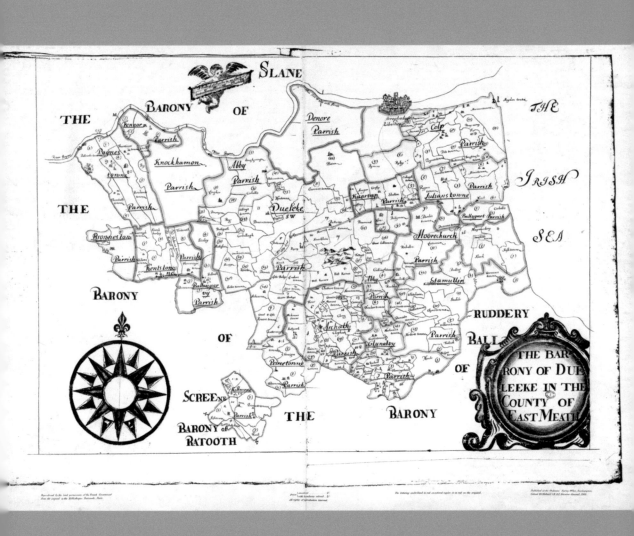

THE BARONY OF SLANE

THE BARONY OF

Kenyor
Parrish
Paynes towne
Knockhamon Parrish
Parrish
Bronnestown
Parrish
Kentstowne
Parrish
Ballsigar by Parrish

Denore Parrish

Abby Parrish

Dueleke
SW

Parrish

Colp
Parrish
Julianstowne
Parrish
Ballypart Parrish
Moorechurch
Parrish
Stamullin
Parrish

Katorcap
Parrish

Abby
Parrish

Arkath
Parrish

Glunaby
Parrish

Painetowne
Parrish

Parrish

RUDDERY
BALL
OF
BARONY

THE BARONY OF EAST MEATH

THE BARONY OF

OF

BARONY OF

SCREENE
Kilmone
Parrish
BARONY of RATOOTH

THE

BARONY

THE BARONY OF DUELEEKE IN THE COUNTY OF EAST MEATH

IRISH SEA

East.Meath County Killaruan

l	— 1	Edwd: Jans Ir:pa:	Killarran	070:0:00
l	— 2		Shallon	240:0:00
l	— 3	Wm: Plunkell Ir:pa:	Grafty	097:2:00
l	— 4	Sym: Luttrell Ir:pa:	Bolloghon . .	111: 1:00
l	— 5	Barth: Moore Ir:p:	Calliaghtowne ..	124:3:00
l	— 6	Wm: Stockes of Misherstowne	Gafney	055:1:00
l	— 7		Anagor	115:3:00
l	— 8	Geo: Tallbott Ir:pa:	Newhaggard ..	121:0:00
l	— 9	Robt: Allen Ir:pa:	Ballgeene . . .	205:0:00
l	— 6 *		ptestant Lands in Gafney . . .	070:0:00

70 : 0 : 00	Earle Anglesey 4		
40 : 0 : 00	E. of Anglesey 4 Robt: Nettervill		⊗
97 : 2 : 00	Earle Anglesey 4		
11 : 1 : 00	Tho : Luttrell 4		
24 : 0 : 00	Geo : Peppard Earle of Anglesey 4		
55 : 1 : 00	Earle of Anglesey 4		
15 : 3 : 00	E: of Anglesey 4		
21 : 0 : 00	Earle of Anglesey 4 Rich.d Tallbott mary Tallbott		
05 : 0 : 00	Ja: & Dame Mary Allen W—	223	Richard Tallbott ⊖ Henry Osborne ⊖
		172ac	Robert Curtis ⊖

...fy DE21

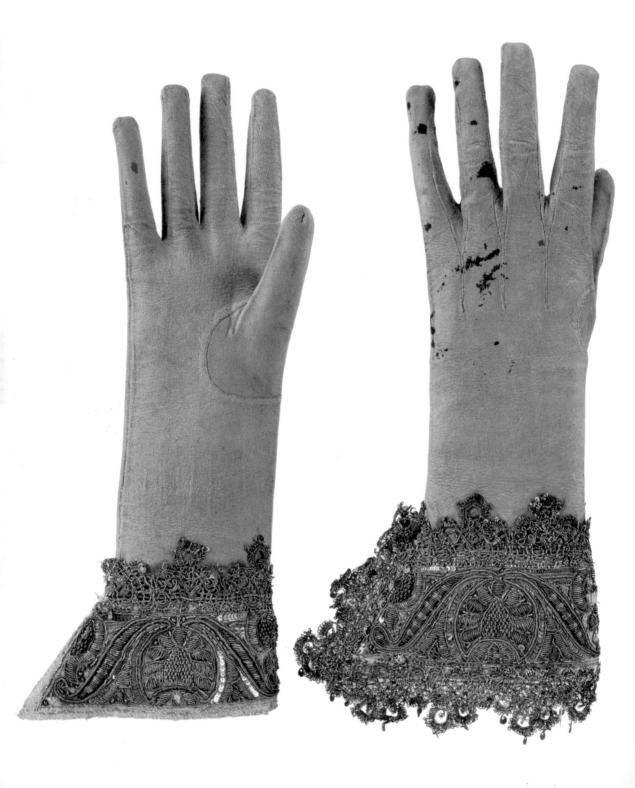

On the morning of 14 July 1690, King William III presented these fine doeskin gloves to John Dillon, in whose home in Lismullin, Co. Meath, he had stayed the previous night. The king had won a major victory over his rival King James II at the nearby River Boyne two days previously. Gloves were often given as presents, but there is reason to think that William may have worn these at the battle, in which he personally commanded the cavalry. William is often depicted wearing heavy, fringed gauntlets such as these in several 'battle' paintings by various artists.

The elaborate gold lace border on the right glove is worn away, and the left glove shows signs of heavy use. If Protestants believed in relics, these remnants of the ultimate hero in his finest hour would surely be holy.

The battle may be the most famous in Irish history, but it was shaped by two events beyond Ireland. One was the succession to the English throne of James II. He alienated parliament and the nobility by his conversion to Catholicism and insistence on the absolute rights of the monarchy. The other event was the French king Louis XIV's invasion of the Rhenish Palatinate and the Netherlands. William of Orange emerged as a key figure in the broad anti-French front that emerged in response. These two issues became one when William, who was James's nephew and son-in-law, arrived in England in November 1688, with 15,000 troops. He and his wife, James's daughter Mary, were crowned king and queen.

James landed in Kinsale in March 1689. His forces failed to establish complete control of the island, with Derry heroically withstanding a siege from April until its relief in August. William followed James to Ireland and hoped for a single decisive battle. The Battle of the Boyne, with 36,000 troops on William's side and 25,000 on James's, was indeed the largest ever fought on Irish soil. It was a pan-European affair, with soldiers from the Netherlands, Denmark, Germany, Norway and Poland, as well as from Britain and Ireland. Frenchmen fought on both sides, with some Huguenot Protestants fighting for William and an army of 6,500 men sent by Louis supporting James.

The decisive action was at the village of Oldbridge. William's flanking manoeuvres drew off most of the Jacobite army, leaving a rump, outnumbered three to one, to face the main attack. The fighting nevertheless lasted for 12 hours, and William's hopes of catching the Jacobites in a pincer movement were dashed. James was able to retreat westwards with the bulk of his army. He escaped to France via Dublin and Cork; most of his Irish army fought on. In that regard, the Boyne was not decisive: the Battle of Aughrim, in July 1691, was far bloodier and more conclusive. Nor was the Boyne the simple sectarian triumph of subsequent legend: William's shock troops, the Dutch Blue Guard, were Catholic, and his allies included the Vatican and Vienna, where *Te Deum*s were sung to celebrate the Boyne victory. Conversely, much of the Protestant hierarchy remained loyal to James. Nevertheless, the personal presence of the two kings gave the Boyne a mythic power that turned it into the ultimate Protestant triumph.

135

WHERE TO SEE THEM: NATIONAL MUSEUM OF IRELAND-DECORATIVE ARTS AND HISTORY, COLLINS BARRACKS, BENBURB STREET, DUBLIN 7; 00-353-1-6777444; WWW.MUSEUM.IE

In 1950, during rebuilding works on an old house in Summerhill in Co. Meath, this rough piece of sandstone was found behind a blocked doorway. It had been in a window recess of a secret, sealed-up chamber. On its face is a carving of the Crucifixion, with the symbols of Christ's Passion and the date 1740. The imagery is vernacular and earthy: the rope used to tie Jesus's hands, the cock that crowed to mark his betrayals by Judas and Peter, the dice thrown by the Roman soldiers, the hammer and pincers used in the Crucifixion and the temple of Jerusalem. The shape of the cross suggests it was based on those sold to pilgrims at Lough Derg.

The stone was clearly used for secret Catholic worship, and its date coincides with one of the first attempts by the state, in 1739–40, to enforce laws penalising Catholicism. It speaks both to the severity of attempts to repress Catholicism and to their failure.

Irish Jacobite resistance, and hopes for a reversal of the transfer of lands from Catholics to Protestants, ended with the Treaty of Limerick in 1691, which seemed to secure Catholics' existing property and religious rights. It promised the same level of tolerance

> as they did enjoy in the reign of King Charles the second: their majesties...will endeavour to procure the said Roman Catholics such farther security...as may preserve them from any disturbance upon the account of their said religion.

Catholic members of the landed gentry who swore allegiance to the new regime could keep their lands.

The Irish parliament refused to comply. Instead, a series of penal laws against Catholics was put in place. The Protestant ascendancy did not regard itself as secure: France remained a threat, as did the papacy's continuing support for the Stuart cause. Some former Jacobites remained active as 'rapparee' or 'tory' outlaws. In 1695, the parliament passed laws prohibiting Catholics from bearing arms without a licence, owning militarily useful horses or travelling to the Continent to be educated.

Gradually, concerns with security became a more nakedly religious project of penalising Catholicism. Laws 'for the suppression of Popery' passed in 1697 and 1703 required bishops, deans, vicars general and friars to leave the country and remaining clergy to register with the authorities; other laws excluded Catholics from parliament, corporations, the army and navy, the legal profession and civic offices; and prevented Catholics from buying land, leasing it for more than 31 years or running schools.

The laws helped to underpin Protestant domination of landholding. The Catholic share of the land fell from 14 per cent in 1702 to 5 per cent by 1776 (many landowning families were converts or crypto-Catholics). In general, the laws were a failure. The majority of the population remained Catholic, and sporadic persecution failed to stop the training of Irish priests in continental seminaries. Catholic worship continued, albeit, as this stone shows, discreetly. The penal laws were evaded, flouted or, if necessary, endured. They did not 'suppress Popery'.

WHERE TO SEE IT: NATIONAL MUSEUM OF IRELAND-DECORATIVE ARTS AND HISTORY, COLLINS BARRACKS, BENBURB STREET, DUBLIN 7; 00-353-1-6777444; WWW.MUSEUM.IE

Conestoga wagons were first made by German immigrants in eastern Pennsylvania in the 1730s. Longer and deeper than European wagons, covered at first with hemp and later with canvas, and having small, manoeuvrable wheels, they were capable of carrying families and heavy freight over rough terrain, making them the ubiquitous vehicle of the push by European settlers westwards across the Appalachian Mountains into the Native American-occupied territories. These wagons also became the characteristic shape of the great migration from Ulster in the half-century after 1718. In all, about 200,000 people left Ulster for colonial America, most of them Presbyterians whose origins lay in Scotland.

This exodus changed both Ireland and America. Here, it affected the balance between the Protestant and Catholic populations. On the other side of the Atlantic, the so-called Ulster Scots or Scotch-Irish destroyed British government efforts to limit the western expansion of the white colony; grabbed huge amounts of Native American land; and became one of the largest components of European settlement in Virginia, Pennsylvania, the Carolinas and Georgia. From the classic image of the frontiersman to country music, and from the populism of Andrew Jackson to evangelical religion, they left a huge imprint on American culture.

Why did they leave Ireland? Presbyterian ministers tended to stress religious persecution as the primary factor—the Test Act of 1704 excluded Presbyterians from public office and ended recog-

nition of their clergy—but economics were almost certainly more important. During the 1710s and late 1720s, Ulster suffered a succession of bad harvests. Leases given in the aftermath of the Williamite victory were running out and landlords sought higher rents. Ulster migrants were not refugees. The lure of free land in America was enhanced by economic discomfort at home.

The Ulster Scots were initially welcomed by the Calvinist communities of New England, but they gradually came to be seen as burdensome and fractious. This, along with their hunger for land, encouraged them to push beyond the established frontiers, bringing them into conflict with a fellow Irishman and convert from Catholicism, William Johnson, who controlled relations between the colonists and the Native American nations. Johnson railed against the Ulster Scots who 'think they do good Service when they Knock an Indian in the Head'. Neither Johnson's efforts nor frequent and bloody conflicts with Native Americans could prevent the push westwards.

Their dynamism and the independent spirit of their Presbyterianism made the Ulster Scots a powerful force in the shaping of an emerging American identity. It is telling that the Declaration of Independence was printed by Tyrone–born John Dunlap; first read in public by John Nixon, a first-generation Ulster Scot; and signed by Charles Thomson, Secretary of the Continental Congress, who was also of Ulster Presbyterian descent.

100 WHERE TO SEE IT: NATIONAL MUSEUMS NORTHERN IRELAND-ULSTER AMERICAN FOLK PARK, 2 MELLON ROAD, CASTLETOWN, OMAGH, CO. TYRONE BT78 5QU; 00-44-845-6080000; WWW.NMNI.COM/UAFP

In 1722, the British government granted English iron manufacturer William Wood permission to proceed with a patent to coin £100,800 worth of copper halfpence for Ireland. The patent had originally been granted to the duchess of Kendal, one of George I's mistresses, who then sold it to Wood for £10,000.

Almost immediately, most of the Dublin establishment was expressing its outrage. There was a widespread belief that the issuing of copper money would devalue Irish coinage and damage the local economy. In July 1722 the archbishop of Dublin, William King, wrote to the lord lieutenant, the duke of Grafton, warning that he found:

> the generality of people here alarmed and greatly dread the consequence of such a project…This is in my opinion a matter of vast consequence both to his Majesty and the subjects for if it be not managed with the utmost caution, it will drain the Kingdom of the little gold and silver that is left in it, and complete the general misery which is already intolerable.

Opposition to the so-called brass money became a rallying cry for both the Protestant establishment and much of the populace of Dublin. There was no challenge to the right of the king to issue coinage, but there was deep resentment at what was seen as exploitation of Ireland. The campaign against Wood's halfpence was blessed, moreover, with the services of a propagandist of genius, Jonathan Swift, dean of St Patrick's Cathedral, who was a great literary ventriloquist. He invented the character of a Dublin 'Drapier' as the author of several open letters attacking the coinage. He also wrote anonymous poetic broadsides. The title of the first, 'A Serious Poem upon William Wood, Grazier, Tinker, Hard-Ware Man, Coiner, Counterfeiter, Founder and Esquire', gives a good flavour of their tone.

The British government under Robert Walpole refused to withdraw the patent. The Dublin parliament, which had been humiliated by the Declaratory Act of 1720—which made it subordinate to Westminster—then sent a resolution to London attacking the coinage. By April 1724 Grafton was replaced as viceroy by Lord Carteret, and a committee of the privy council recommended that the amount of coinage issued be reduced to £40,000. These concessions were accompanied by an insistence from London that 'the affair of the coinage was now come to be an affair of State wherein the honour of the King and the English Nation were more materially concerned'. The halfpence had become a point of principle for both sides. In the end the government capitulated. In August 1725 Wood's patent was withdrawn—he was secretly compensated with a pension of £3,000 a year from Irish revenues.

The affair marked the emergence of a strain of Protestant 'patriotism', one that did not seek to include Catholics as citizens but did insist on the idea of Ireland as an independent and equal kingdom. 'You ARE', wrote Swift's Drapier, 'and OUGHT to be as FREE a People as your Brethren in England'. It was a notion that would have an ambiguous life in Protestant Ireland but eventually a more potent one in America.

140

By the terms of the treaties of Galway (22 July 1691) and Limerick (3 October 1691) that ended Jacobite resistance in Ireland, members of the defeated army were allowed to enter the service of Catholic powers on the continent. About 20,000 went immediately to France, and over the first half of the eighteenth century the so-called Wild Geese continued to seek their fortunes in the armies of France, Spain and Austria. The numbers were not large, some 6,500 between 1716 and 1791, but, especially for the sons of dispossessed Catholic landowners, foreign military service acted as a way of clinging to a lost status.

Dillon's Regiment was unique—it was continuously under the command of members of the same family for more than a century. It was first raised to fight for James II in 1688 by Theobald Dillon, who was killed at Aughrim. In 1691 it was part of the Irish brigade that joined the French army, and served in Piedmont and Savoy. It also served at the capture of Barcelona in 1697 and the defence of Cremona in 1702. The most famous battle in which the regiment and the larger Irish brigade took part was at Fontenoy, near Tournai in Belgium in May 1745, at which this flag was flown. This was a crucial episode in the war of 1740–48, when France and Prussia clashed with Britain and the Netherlands over who would succeed Charles VI of Austria.

The French, under the Marechal de Saxe, were losing to the Anglo-Dutch force under the duke of Cumberland when 4,000 men of the Irish brigade counter-attacked with the cry of 'Remember Limerick'. The butchery at Fontenoy achieved little in the long-term: the war eventually ended with roughly the same balance of power as existed at its beginning. Nevertheless, Fontenoy was idealised, especially on its centenary, as a glorious Irish victory over England.

The male descendants of former Jacobite landowners proved to be remarkably adept adventurers. Some joined the British imperial service: Peter Warren, from a Jacobite crypto-Catholic family in Co. Meath, joined the British navy and made his fortune from captured Spanish ships and astute American trading, founding Greenwich Village in New York. His nephew William Johnson left Meath for the wilds of upstate New York in the 1730s and ended up as both a Mohawk chief and a British baronet. On the other side of the fence, Sir Charles Wogan acted as the most dashing fixer for the Stuart pretenders, ending up as a senator of Rome and governor of La Mancha, in Spain.

The figure of the swaggering officer returned from continental wars epitomised a strain of Catholic male pride. In her great 'Lament for Art O'Leary', Eibhlín Dubh Ní Chonaill recalls her husband, a captain in the Austrian army, with his 'silver-hilted' sword, fine horse and elegant clothes: the very image of the uppity Catholic. In truth, the Wild Geese were more of a safety valve than a threat to the established order. The Irish Brigade was disbanded in 1783 as part of the peace between France and Britain after the American war. Ironically, in 1792, in the aftermath of the French Revolution, the remnants of the Dillon regiment joined the British army.

143

WHERE TO SEE IT: NATIONAL MUSEUM OF IRELAND-DECORATIVE ARTS AND HISTORY, COLLINS BARRACKS, BENBURB STREET, DUBLIN 7; 00-353-1-6777444; WWW.MUSEUM.IE

70. ROCOCO SILVER CANDLESTICK, *c*.1745

With its wild floral elaborations and flamboyant abandonment of symmetry or straight lines, this candlestick is characteristic of the rococo style that became the rage in Paris in the 1720s. That it was made in Dublin tells us something both about the extravagant taste of the Irish ruling class and about the city itself.

Members of the ascendancy could spend enormous sums on silver plate. A dinner service commissioned by the earl of Kildare in 1745, the year when our candlestick was probably made, cost £4,044 at a time when £44 would have been a comfortable annual middle-class income. The 'family silver' was a crucial token of status, and the over-the-top rococo style was perfect for the flaunting of wealth. Much of the silver made in Dublin was a local version of a London take on a Parisian original—Huguenot craftsmen fleeing the persecution of Protestants in France forming one of the networks through which styles were diffused. Dublin silverware, made by masters such as John Hamilton and Robert Calderwood, was not, however, merely provincial: it attained very high levels of artistry and came to be prized for itself.

That Dublin could produce such objects is a token of its remarkable development. At the end of the Cromwellian wars, the city was small and miserable: Cromwell described its castle as 'the worst in Christendom', and its two cathedrals were virtually falling down. Its population was just 9,000. Yet, over the following century, Dublin came to be regarded as the second city of the British Empire.

The Protestant ruling class felt secure enough to invest in the radical redevelopment of its capital city. Beginning with Parliament House, on College Green, in 1728, a series of grand buildings was erected, including the Royal Exchange and James Gandon's Custom House and Four Courts. The mediaeval streetscape was transformed with the creation of fine squares and wide thoroughfares. Intellectual life blossomed, with figures such as Jonathan Swift, George Berkeley, Richard Steele, the Sheridan family and Mary Delany giving the city an international cultural status. The first performance of George Frideric Handel's 'Messiah' at Fishamble Street Theatre in 1742 was a mark of Dublin's new stature.

For the rich, Lord Cloncurry's claim that Dublin was 'one of the most agreeable places of residence in Europe' had substance. The contrast with the squalor of the city's poor was, however, stark. With little or no sanitation, gross overcrowding, intermittent famine and epidemic disease, low wages and high unemployment, it is unsurprising that Dublin was infamous for its beggars.

Child poverty and child mortality reached appalling levels: 25,000 children were taken in by Dublin Foundling Hospital between 1784 and 1796; more than 17,000 subsequently died. Dublin, for all, its elegance, mirrored the profound divisions between the ruling elite and the impoverished majority that were a feature of the *ancien regime* world.

WHERE TO SEE IT: NATIONAL MUSEUM OF IRELAND-DECORATIVE ARTS AND HISTORY, COLLINS BARRACKS, BENBURB ST, DUBLIN 7; 00-353-1-6777444; WWW.MUSEUM.IE

Plate VI.   Wm Hincks Ind.t & Sculp.

1 Spinning
2 Reeling
3 Reeling the
  Yarn or Thread

To the RIGHT HON.^{BLE} *The* EARL *of* MOIRA,

THIS Plate, TAKEN ON THE SPOT IN THE COUNTY OF DOWNE,

Representing Spinning, Reeling with the Clock Reel, and Boiling the Yarn,

Is most respectfully Dedicated by his Lordships much obliged & humble Servant, Wm Hincks.

Published as the Act directs   London Augt 3^d 1783 by Wm Hincks.

71. ENGRAVING OF LINEN-MAKERS, 1782

This engraving, one of a set of twelve by Irish artist William Hincks, is a rare artefact: it acknowledges the work of women. It is, as the title explains, a view 'taken on the spot in the County of Downe, Representing Spinning, Reeling with the Clock reel, and Boiling the Yarn'. The work was hard, but the relative prosperity of the cottage depicted in the engraving hints at the enormous impact the linen trade had on Irish standards of living in the eighteenth century. Irish people had been growing flax and making linen since the Bronze Age. With Ireland largely pacified in the early-eighteenth century, the authorities promoted the development of linen as the primary Irish industry. The wool industry was discouraged to avoid competition with England, and linen was an unthreatening substitute.

The Linen Board was formed with public money in Dublin in 1711 to regulate the growing industry. In the second half of the century production expanded dramatically, and by 1800 linen exports had risen to between 35 million and 40 million yards. Early linen production was not industrialised. It centred on farm-family units, with the whole household involved in planting and harvesting the flax, the women and girls spinning it into yarn and the men weaving the yarn into cloth.

Linen had a particularly dramatic effect on the economy of Ulster, transforming a hitherto poor province into the most prosperous in Ireland. Initially, the trade was centred on the Linen Hall, which opened on Dublin's north side in 1728; the Ulster origins of much of the cloth was acknowledged in the surrounding street names: Coleraine, Lurgan, Lisburn. Gradually, however, Ulster traders took control of the export business and Belfast Linen Hall opened in 1783. In the 'linen triangle' between Lisburn, Dungannon and Armagh in particular linen drapers formed a new entrepreneurial nexus, typically Presbyterian and often open to radical ideas, especially during and after the American Revolution.

Linen transformed Ulster in other ways too. Hunger for land to grow flax led to the destruction of the last of the great Ulster forests that had terrified Tudor armies: the last wolf in the Sperrin Mountains was killed in the 1760s. The population rose rapidly: between 1753 and 1791 the number of households paying hearth tax in Ulster doubled. Market and estate towns such as Banbridge, Downpatrick and Newtownards were redeveloped. This rapid change produced new social tensions, including militant protests in 1771–2 by groups called the Hearts of Oak and Hearts of Steel, enraged by bad harvests, taxes and rent rises. Emigration to Colonial America peaked in the 1770s; in the 1780s sectarian tensions rose, especially in Co. Armagh, now the most populous county in Ireland, where the Protestant Peep O'Day Boys and the Catholic Defenders engaged in low-level warfare. These tensions were fuelled, ironically, by the very success of the linen trade, as Catholic and Protestant weavers competed for business.

WHERE TO SEE IT: NATIONAL MUSEUMS NORTHERN IRELAND-ULSTER MUSEUM, BOTANIC GARDENS, BELFAST BT9 5AB; 00-44-845-6080000; WWW.NMNI.COM/UM

72. COTTON PANEL
SHOWING VOLUNTEER REVIEW, 1783

In November 1783 Edward Clarke, proprietor of the Irish Furniture, Cotton and Linen Warehouse on Werburgh Street in Dublin, advertised for sale:

> a Volunteer furniture, with an exact representation of the Last Provincial Review in Phoenix Park, with a striking likeness of Lord Charlemont as reviewing General.

That images of the Volunteers, like this one, produced by Thomas Harpur in Leixlip, were desirable consumer goods for the well-to-do is vivid evidence of the political ferment of the decade.

Volunteering took off in 1778, as a response to the American War of Independence. France joined the war on the side of the colonists, and there were fears it might attempt to invade Ireland. Regiments of regular troops were sent to fight in America, leaving the administration with little choice but to accommodate the formation of Volunteer corps. As Lord Charlemont, the commander-in-chief depicted on the panel, put it: 'They feared and consequently hated the Volunteers, yet to them alone they looked for... safety'. By late 1779, 40,000 men were under arms, half of them in Ulster.

Charlemont was also the leader of the so-called Patriot Connexion in the Irish House of Lords, and an ally of opposition leaders Henry Flood and Henry Grattan. This faction was not innately revolutionary, taking Ireland's connection to Britain for granted. Nevertheless, it wanted more local control over Irish affairs, and the re-moval of Westminster's restrictions on Irish trade. It especially opposed two pieces of legislation. Poynings' Law (1494) allowed the privy council in London to veto or alter legislation passed by the (entirely Protestant) Irish parliament. The Declaratory Act (1720) gave Westminster the right (rarely used) to legislate for Irish affairs.

In 1779, after demonstrations by the armed Volunteers outside the parliament on College Green, London lifted restrictions on the export of wool, glass and other goods from Ireland. Success bred larger demands: in February 1782, the Volunteer convention in Dungannon approved resolutions demanding legislative and judicial independence for Ireland and further relaxation of the Penal Laws. In May the dismantling of the Penal Laws was intensified, and in June the Declaratory Act was repealed and Poynings' Law amended. The Volunteers, and their liberal Protestant supporters, then faced the hardest question of all: what about middle-class Protestants and the Catholic majority? Belfast and Dublin radicals pushed for an extensive widening of the franchise, for Catholics as well as Protestants; conservatives in parliament and the Volunteers took fright. Reform was rejected and the Volunteers began to decline.

The French Revolution of 1789 upped the stakes. The Belfast Volunteers hailed it as 'the Hope of this World'. Establishment liberals drew back from the cause of 'liberty'. The gulf between radicalism and reaction became even wider, and for both sides the stakes seemed even higher.

100 WHERE TO SEE IT: NATIONAL MUSEUM OF IRELAND-DECORATIVE ARTS AND HISTORY, COLLINS BARRACKS, BENBURB STREET, DUBLIN 7; 00-353-1-6777444, WWW.MUSEUM.IE

No Irish event of such consequence is more powerfully symbolised by a single object than the 1798 insurrection and the pike. Pikes were a standard weapon of mediaeval and early modern armies, but by the eighteenth century they were much more strongly associated with revolutionary violence. So symbolic of popular insurrection has the weapon become that it is generally forgotten that crown forces in Ireland in 1798 also used pikes.

The first seizure of hidden pikes was in Dublin in 1793. Four years later the directory of the Society of United Irishmen ordered all members who could not afford firearms to equip themselves with pikes. More than 70,000 were found in government searches in Leinster and Ulster in 1797 alone. When fighting finally began, charges by massed ranks of pike-wielding men were the main rebel tactic. Jonah Barrington, an independent observer, noted 'the extreme expertise with which the Irish handled the pike'. Even this expertise was seldom sufficient for very long against trained troops.

The United Irishmen, founded in Belfast in October 1791, aimed, as one of its leaders, Theobald Wolfe Tone, put it, to 'comprehensively embrace Irishmen of all denominations' in the cause of democratic reform and 'national government'. Its initial methods were constitutional, but after Britain declared war on revolutionary France in 1793, demands for peaceful reform were increasingly met with frustration and repression, culminating in the banning of the United Irishmen. Campaigns for reform turned to dreams of revolution. Tone and other leaders went to Paris to lobby the revolutionary government for support. A French invasion fleet of 43 ships set sail for Bantry Bay in December 1796 but was driven back by gales.

Thereafter, the government launched a ferocious campaign of repression, aimed at disarming the would-be rebels. Through house-burnings, floggings, executions and torture, it smashed the United Irish organisation in Ulster, which had deep support among Presbyterians. While Tone waited for another French invasion, the United Irish at home planned to go ahead with a rebellion, which took hold mostly in Wexford and Wicklow. By the end of May 1798 the rebels had taken Wexford town and Enniscorthy. They were driven back from New Ross on 4 June, however, and crushed at Vinegar Hill above Enniscorthy on 21 June. A belated rising in Ulster, beginning in Antrim on 7 June and partly led by young Belfast cotton-maker Henry Joy McCracken, had also been defeated. By the time a small French force under General Jean-Joseph Humbert arrived at Killala Bay, in Mayo, on 22 August, it was no more than a bloody coda to one of the bloodiest episodes in Irish history. When Tone, captured on a French ship, took his own life, he was one of perhaps 30,000 who had died violently since May.

The United Irishmen's hope for a non-sectarian Irish democracy was drowned in this bloodshed; the conflict ultimately reinforced sectarian divisions by shattering Presbyterian radicalism. The idea of 'the pike in the thatch' retained its romantic appeal, but 1798 changed Ireland for good: the revolutionaries' ideal of unity became an ever more distant dream.

151

WHERE TO SEE IT: NATIONAL MUSEUM OF IRELAND-DECORATIVE ARTS AND HISTORY, COLLINS BARRACKS, BENBURB STREET, DUBLIN 7; 00-353-1-6777444, WWW.MUSEUM.IE

74. ACT OF UNION BLACKLIST, EARLY-NINETEENTH CENTURY

This list, written out in this instance by barrister and writer Jonah Barrington, circulated in a number of manuscript copies in the early-nineteenth century. (Just one page of nineteen is shown here.) On one side of the page are the names of members of the Irish parliament in 1799. On the other are the rewards they received for voting in favour of the Act of Union, which abolished Ireland's independent status and created the United Kingdom of Great Britain and Ireland.

> Richard Hare, put two members into Parliament, and was created Lord Ennismore for their votes…Colonel Heniker, a regiment, and paid £3,500 for his seat by the Commissioners of Compensation…got a peerage;…George Hatton, appointed Commissioner of Stamps; J. Hutchinson, a general, Lord Hutchinson; Hugh Howard, Lord Wicklow's brother, made Postmaster General; William Handcock, Athlone, (an extraordinary instance; he made and sang songs against the Union in 1799, at a public dinner of the Opposition, and made and sang songs for it in 1800); he got a peerage…Hon. G. Jocelyn, promotion in the Army, and his brother consecrated bishop of Lismore.

The decision to move rapidly ahead with a full union was London's response to the violence of 1798 and to the continuing war with France. Prime Minister William Pitt imagined the union as the only way to draw Catholics into loyalty—a matter of increasing urgency given that one-third of the British army was Irish. The lure was to be Catholic emancipation and the abolition of an exclusively Protestant and generally reactionary Irish parliament. At Westminster, Irish playwright and radical Richard Brinsley Sheridan attacked British treatment of Ireland. Pitt, remarkably, conceded that British policy 'tainted and perverted by selfish notions treated Ireland with illiberality and neglect'. The implication was that union would prevent the ascendancy from pursuing that 'selfish' interest.

Meanwhile, the Irish Catholic bishops secretly adopted resolutions in favour of accepting state salaries for clergy and a government veto on the nomination of bishops. But would the Dublin parliament abolish itself? In January 1799 the chief secretary concluded, in the face of a hostile Irish House of Commons, that 'the measure could not be proceeded with until the mood of the country changed'. In March many Orange lodges passed resolutions against the union. Faced with such opposition, the government resorted to wholesale bribery: the secret service was limited to expenditure of £5,000 domestically but spent £32,336 in buying votes for the union. On 6 February 1800, the House of Commons in Dublin voted for union by 158 votes to 115. On 1 August the Act of Union became law, to come into effect on 1 January 1801. Oliver MacDonagh called it 'the most important single factor in shaping Ireland as a nation in the modern world'. Officially, the two islands now contained 'one people'. It was hoped they would enjoy equal treatment under the law.

WHERE TO SEE IT: NATIONAL LIBRARY OF IRELAND, KILDARE STREET, DUBLIN 2; 00-353-1-6030200; WWW.NLI.IE

55. Colonel B. Henniker . dead. { A Regiment and paid £3.500 for his seat by the Commissioners of Compensation.

56 Peter Holmes, ... dead. A Commissioner of Stamps.

57 George Hatton . . . . . dead. Appointed Commissioner of Stamps

58 Hon John Hutchinson . . A General. Lord Hutchinson

59 Hugh Howard . . . . . dead { Lord Wicklow's Brother made Post master General.

60 William Handcock (Athlone) { An extraordinary instance, he made and sang songs against the Union in 1799, at a public dinner of the opposition, and made and sang songs for it in 1800. he got a Peerage.

61 John Hobson . dead. { Appointed Store Keeper at the Castle Ordnance

7

This glass decanter is striking for its elegance of form and luxurious, almost sensual curves. Its applied cutting is a variant of the more typical style of semi-circular pendant arch motif, with a star underneath and pillars running around it—typical of the work of the Penrose glass factory in Waterford. It also tells a poignant story: the flowering of an Irish industry in the two decades before the Act of Union and its withering after.

The Penroses were representative of the more dynamic, entrepreneurial side of Anglo-Ireland. With roots in Cornwall, they moved to Ireland in 1656, by which time they may already have been Quakers. William Penrose established himself in Waterford in the early-eighteenth century as a tanner and merchant, and his son, also William, founded the Waterford Glass Factory in 1783. It cost £10,000 to establish and employed between 50 and 70 workers, especially cutters and engravers. It can be seen as an excellent example of positive Anglo-Irish relations: the immensely skilled John Hill, who oversaw the process, was a Quaker brought from Stourbridge, in Worcestershire, taking eight or ten of the 'best set of workmen' with him. Their skills, passed on to Irish workers, quickly earned Waterford glass a high international reputation: Penrose products were sold in the United States, Canada, the West Indies, France, Spain and Portugal. Irish-made glass, including that from Waterford, also began to replace imports.

The Penrose factory was made possible by the lifting of English prohibitions on the export of glass from Ireland and of duties on coal used for its manufacture in the dynamic 1780s. The Act of Union should not have interfered with the business, which was carried on by Jonathan Gathchell after the Penroses gave it up on William's death, in 1799. Initially, indeed, the glass industry continued to thrive in Waterford, Cork, Dublin, Belfast and Newry. Westminster, however, often proved indifferent if not hostile to Irish commercial interests. In 1811 flint glass made in Ireland and exported was made liable to duty; in 1825 a very heavy excise tax was imposed on glass manufacturers, which devastated the industry in Ireland. Ireland had eleven glass factories that year, and by 1852 it had only two: one in Belfast and one in Dublin. The Waterford glass factory had closed in 1851. In the previous decade overall employment in the making of pottery and glass in Ireland had fallen by 45 per cent.

The decline of the glass industry is part of a larger pattern: the failure of Ireland under the union to catch up with the British industrial revolution. If anything, Irish industry declined. Historians dispute the causes and nature of 'de-industrialisation', and it was a gradual process. What is clear is that industrial employment became increasingly dependent on the textile sector, which was heavily concentrated in the north. In 1841 about 32 per cent of the labour force was in industry, but of the industrial workforce, about two-thirds were in textiles, chiefly linen. Unity with a great industrial power did not prevent Ireland beyond Ulster from becoming, over the course of the nineteenth century, a more agricultural society.

100 WHERE TO SEE IT: NATIONAL MUSEUM OF IRELAND-DECORATIVE ARTS AND HISTORY, COLLINS BARRACKS, BENBURB STREET, DUBLIN 7; 00-353-1-6777444; WWW.MUSEUM.IE

The emerald stone in this ring may symbolise imperialism: it came from India and was given by Sir John Temple to his cousin Dr Robert Emmet, the Irish state physician. The design, cut in Dublin in the 1790s, symbolises something very different: Hibernia playing a harp, with, in the background, pikes and a liberty cap—emblems of Irish republicanism. The ring, which seems to have been copied, was used by Emmet's revolutionary sons, Thomas Addis and Robert, as a seal and apparently as a token of trust. Myles Byrne, a fellow conspirator in the United Irishmen, recalls meeting Thomas Addis in Paris and giving him

> a paper containing the impression of the seal-ring which I had been the bearer of from his brother, Robert. As soon as Mr Emmet had compared this impression with his own seal-ring, he crossed the room, took me in his arms and embraced me with affection.

Thomas Addis Emmet was among the United Irish leaders interned in Fort George, in Scotland, in 1799 and released in 1802. His younger brother Robert was expelled from Trinity College Dublin in 1798, rightly suspected of radical activities. Robert went to Paris and discussed with Napoleon (now established as a dictator) and his foreign minister Charles Talleyrand the possibility of a new rebellion, this time focused on the capture of Dublin Castle, the centre of government power. Robert returned to Dublin in 1802, determined to put this plan into effect. He was in some respects a romantic idealist, but his military ambitions were real. He hoped to link up with a rump of rebels from 1798 who were holding out in the Wicklow hills under Michael Dwyer. He also planned to use more sophisticated technology: hinged pikes that could be more easily hidden, short muskets for urban street fighting and signal rockets that he test-fired in the spring of 1803. Emmet and his co-conspirators also developed something that would play a significant role in Irish and world history: the improvised explosive device.

Emmet succeeded in catching the government by surprise with his plans for the rebellion, fixed for 23 July, but seems to have done the same with his own men, many of whom were also unprepared. Most of those who gathered in Dublin on the day lost faith in their youthful commander and returned home, and instead of the 1,000 strong army that Emmet had been expecting, he ended up leading a drunken rabble of 80.

Emmet sent a rocket signal to countermand the rising, which nonetheless unfolded as a confused melée, in which the lord chief justice, Lord Kilwarden, was piked to death. Emmet and much of the leadership withdrew into the south Dublin hills, but Emmet was arrested in Harold's Cross on 25 August, taken to the castle, tried on 19 September and executed on Thomas Street the following day.

Emmet's youth (he was 25 at the time of his death) and idealism, his dramatic parting from his beloved Sarah Curran, the disappearance of his body and his speech from the dock—'when my country takes her place among the nations of the earth, then, and not till then, let my epitaph be written'—created a myth of heroism and blood sacrifice that lived long after him.

WHERE TO SEE IT: NATIONAL MUSEUM OF IRELAND-DECORATIVE ARTS AND HISTORY, COLLINS BARRACKS, BENBURB STREET, DUBLIN 7; 00-353-1-6777444; WWW.MUSEUM.IE

This cradle, woven from wicker, was collected on Inis Óirr, one of the Aran Islands, in the 1950s, but it is probably much older and is of a type widely used in nineteenth-century Ireland. That it was made with such loving skill suggests both its necessity and its importance. Ordinary Irish people experienced in an extreme way both the joys of having children and the pain of losing them.

In the early-nineteenth century the population in Ireland was growing faster than anywhere else in western Europe. In 1807 Thomas Malthus wrote that 'Among the subjects peculiar to the state of Ireland is the extraordinary phenomenon of the very rapid increase of its population'. At the end of the eighteenth century the population was probably about 5 million; by 1845 it had risen to about 8.5 million. By 1845 31 per cent of the entire population of the United Kingdom lived in Ireland. This is all the more remarkable given that, between 1815 and 1845, about 1.5 million people left Ireland, mostly for Britain, Canada and the United States.

Love was in the air because the almost universal adoption of the potato as a staple crop made it possible to form a family with very little land. The potato, which was something of a wonder food, may also have contributed to the general good health of Irish women and, therefore, their very high fertility. (It is striking that high fertility in Ireland was not just a Catholic phenomenon: Quakers in pre-famine rural Ireland had more children than those in rural England.) Irish women were also sexually conservative—generally chaste before marriage and faithful within it—and few seemed to have used birth control. Children, moreover, were welcomed, as they often are in poor societies, as an insurance policy for their parents' futures. English agronomist Arthur Young noted, of the Irish poor, 'their happiness and ease relative to the number of children'. Up to the 1820s, when cottage industries began to be wiped out by competition from factories, children were valuable workers in the home.

Furthermore, the cost of an extra mouth was minimal: families had little to give a child beyond the food they grew themselves. Because of the failure of most parts of Ireland to industrialise, the number of smallholdings grew disproportionately: in 1845, 55 per cent of all Irish landholders held farms of less than four hectares (10 acres), and another 20 per cent of farms were smaller than eight hectares (20 acres). In addition to the problem of having so many subsistence farmers, Ireland was becoming more unequal: while overall incomes were rising modestly, the poor were getting poorer. In 1835 the Poor Inquiry Commission asked local Catholic and Protestant clergy, magistrates and land agents to say whether the condition of the poor in their area had improved or disimproved since the end of the Napoleonic Wars, in 1815. Most reported a deterioration. Perhaps a quarter of children died in infancy, making the cradle a bittersweet object, redolent both of hope and of loss.

159

WHERE TO SEE IT: NATIONAL MUSEUM OF IRELAND-DECORATIVE ARTS AND HISTORY, COLLINS BARRACKS, BENBURB STREET, DUBLIN 7; 00-353-1-6777444; WWW.MUSEUM.IE

In September 1844, this extravagantly ornate 'chariot' was drawn through the streets of Dublin by six splendid grey horses, accompanied by a crowd of around 200,000 citizens. Sitting on the gilded seat was the most celebrated, adored, feared and despised Irishman of his time: Daniel O'Connell. He was being taken from Richmond Bridewell, on the site of what became Griffith barracks in Dublin, to his home on Merrion Square.

O'Connell, his son John and others were found guilty on conspiracy charges after a 24-day trial that opened on 15 January 1844. They were sentenced to twelve months in prison, fined £2,000 and bonded to keep the peace for seven years. On 4 September, however, the House of Lords overturned the verdict. The 'chariot', 3 metres high and 4.5 metres long, was specially made for O'Connell's glorious re-entry into the city, and modelled on the triumphal cars of ancient Rome. It was upholstered in purple silk and blue wool and adorned with gilded mouldings and decorative overlays, depicting shamrocks and stylised classical foliage. The sides showed Hibernia with the increasingly familiar national iconography of harp, round tower and wolfhound. On the back was a representation in gold of a harp surmounted by the word 'Repeal', summarising O'Connell's campaign for repeal of the Act of Union.

O'Connell was a political phenomenon, with good claims to be the inventor of mass democracy, not just in Ireland but around the English-speaking world. His first great cause was Catholic emancipation. It had been widely believed that the quid pro quo for the union would be a lifting of the remaining legal disabilities for Catholics, including the right to sit in parliament, but opposition from George III and then from his son blocked reform. O'Connell, a barrister and member of the Dublin Catholic Committee, built the Catholic Association as a mass movement, funded by the 'Catholic rent'—monthly subscriptions of as little as a penny. In July 1828 he won a historic election in Clare by 2,057 votes to 982. In April 1829, the Roman Catholic Relief Act enabled Catholics to enter parliament and hold high civil and military offices.

O'Connell, now known as the 'Liberator', achieved a status unique in the world: political authority without institutional power. French writer Gustave de Beaumont noted in 1839 that:

> what we find nowhere else is the continued empire of a single man, who during 20 years has reigned over his country without any title, save popular assent, every day required and every day given… his power is only maintained on the condition of incessant action; hence that feverish agitation by which he is distinguished.

O'Connell's agitation encompassed the rights of Jews and American slaves, but focused primarily on repeal. His campaign failed; but it put Ireland at the centre of British politics and created a politicised population whose skills would help shape politics, not only in Ireland, but in Britain and the US.

WHERE TO SEE IT: DERRYNANE HOUSE, CAHERDANIEL, CO. KERRY; 00-353-66-9475113; WWW.HERITAGEIRELAND.IE/EN/SOUTH-WEST/DERRYNANEHOUSE/

This remarkable table cloth, measuring eight feet by four and showing 250 different figures in 31 panels of inlaid felt patchwork, is the work of one man over 20 years. Stephen Stokes was born in Plymouth in 1802 and enlisted in the army as a boy. In 1819 he entered the 63rd Regiment, then stationed in Ireland, transferring to the 1st Royal Dragoons in 1826. On leaving the army in 1836 he joined the newly formed Dublin Metropolitan Police (DMP), initially as a sergeant. He retired as inspector of mounted police in 1855 and became superintendent of the Turkish baths in Lincoln Place. He died in 1900 at the age of 98.

Stokes seems to have been self-taught and presumably began his project to stave off the boredom of barracks life. His patchwork evolved into a panorama of political, military and even cultural affairs. At the centre are Queen Victoria and Prince Albert reviewing the troops, the royal coat of arms and a vivid depiction of the capture of a French standard at the Battle of Waterloo in 1815 by the 1st Royal Dragoons, presumably described to Stokes by colleagues in the regiment who were veterans of that epic clash.

The real fascination of the patchwork, though, lies in its scenes from ordinary military life and from very different aspects of Irish affairs. Running across the width of the cloth, there is a funeral procession for a dead dragoon. Another sequence shows soldiers being punished for breaches of discipline by having to break rocks or march with a heavy wheelbarrow, all supervised by a provost marshal with an enormous pipe. A later panel shows a member of the DMP mounting a white horse—possibly Stokes himself.

There are contrasting scenes from Irish life. One is of Donnybrook fair, a proverbially riotous annual gathering south of Dublin. Another is the visit of the celebrated 'Swedish nightingale', Jenny Lind, to the Theatre Royal in Dublin in 1847. For the following year, however, Stokes depicts 'The Irish Constabulary and the Boys of Ballingarry', representing the abortive 1848 rebellion of the Young Irelanders. This group, a violent breakaway from the mainstream repeal movement, had serious ambitions and approached the French revolutionary government. After two of its leaders, John Mitchel and Charles Gavan Duffy, were arrested, about 100 members engaged in a desultory skirmish with 40 policemen in Co. Tipperary, an engagement derisively known as 'the battle of the Widow McCormack's cabbage-patch'. William Smith O'Brien, Terence Bellew McManus, Thomas Francis Meagher and Patrick O'Donohue were sentenced to death but were instead transported to Van Diemen's Land in 1849.

Stokes's depiction of the 'battle' is striking for two reasons: he shows the rebels as giants compared to the diminutive policemen; and he gives prominence to a very early depiction of the rebels' flag: a tricolour of green, white and orange. Brought from Paris, where it was displayed to show the Young Irelanders' affinity for the French revolution, it symbolised, said Meagher, the hope that 'beneath its folds the hands of the Irish Catholic and the Irish Protestant may be clasped in generous and heroic brotherhood'—an aspiration yet to be fulfilled.

163

100 WHERE TO SEE IT: NATIONAL MUSEUM OF IRELAND-DECORATIVE ARTS AND HISTORY, COLLINS BARRACKS, BENBURB STREET, DUBLIN 7; 00-353-1-6777444; WWW.MUSEUM.IE

One of the great hidden objects of Irish history is the threatening letter. For a burgeoning population of very poor tenants, Daniel O'Connell's campaigns for Catholic emancipation and repeal of the Act of Union had less urgency than matters that bore on their immediate survival: rent, land tenure and the tithes that were extorted from Catholics to pay Church of Ireland clergymen. For much of the nineteenth century, the most violent resistance of the anonymous poor was personified in a single, mythical figure, Captain Rock, whose name was appended to thousands of threatening letters, like this one sent to Thomas Larcom, the chief surveyor of Ireland, in 1842.

Secret, oath-bound societies, generally known as Ribbonmen, survived the repression of the 1798 rising. Liberal republicanism was largely eclipsed in their ideology by a millenarian and sectarian fervour crystallised in an exotic word: Pastorini, the pen name of Bishop Charles Walmesley, whose reading of the Book of Revelation led him to predict in the 1770s that God's wrath would punish Protestant heretics in 50 years time. During an outbreak of famine and fever in 1817, condensed versions of Pastorini's prophecies began to circulate among rural Irish Catholics. The idea that Protestants would be wiped out by 1825 gained a powerful hold.

A Co. Limerick blacksmith called Patrick Dillane, distinguished in the art of throwing rocks, was 'christened Captain Rock by a schoolmaster… by pouring a glass of wine on his head'. The name became a code for the sense that, as a Rockite puts it in a story by William Carleton, 'we'll have our own agin'.

Rockism swept through Munster and south Leinster between 1821 and 1824, with savagely violent attacks on landlords, agents, tithe collectors, and middlemen. More than 1000 people were murdered, mutilated or badly beaten. The millenarian fervour was evident in threatening letters containing phrases like the exuberantly apocalyptic 'Vesuvius or Etna never sent forth such crackling flames as some parts of Donoughmore will shortly emit'. (The letters were not at times without a certain grotesque humour: 'In compassion to your human weaknesses and in consideration of the enormous weight of your corpulent fraim [sic], I mean to rid you of these inconveniences by a decapitation'.)

At its height in North Cork, Rockism could bring thousands of men and women into open insurrectionary action against troops and yeomanry. The Rockites won no military victories, but their campaign of arson and murder did succeed in cowing local magistrates, stopping the collection of tithes and lowering rents. The intimidation of witnesses and 'informers' created a period of virtual legal immunity.

It took large-scale military occupations, mass hangings, transportations and the introduction of the brutal Insurrection Act, suspending civil liberties (most of those sentenced were accused of nothing more than breaking the curfew), to end Captain Rock's three-year reign of terror. Even then, the memory of the violence was evoked in subsequent decades, as this letter shows, to threaten unpopular landlords or officials with a name that remained charged with ferocity.

WHERE TO SEE IT: NATIONAL LIBRARY OF IRELAND, KILDARE STREET, DUBLIN 2; 00-353-1-6030200; WWW.NLI.IE

Stales

If You do not leave your situation

against Saturday, the 3 of July, you
shall have a visit from Captain Rock
We would wait on your father the
blody orange man but that he
is two old but we are determined
to visit you and if you do not
leave cok to the bottom of this
letter we write at the same time
to Larkum threatning him with
the same fait

You have till the 3
to have your life

Capt Rock
Rock hall

81. EMPTY COOKING POT, NINETEENTH CENTURY

For the Irish rural poor, the open fireplace of a small stone cottage was the locus of comfort and security. Suspended over the turf fire was a large, three-legged, iron cooking pot. By the nineteenth century, these vessels were almost always mass manufactured in a style that harked back to mediaeval times; they continued in use until the mid-twentieth century—this six-gallon example, from Corelish East, Grean, Co. Limerick, was purchased by the National Museum in 1965. These pots became a talisman of survival. Folklorist Estyn Evans noted that during the years of the Great Hunger—the potato famine of 1845–9—victims 'clung to the pot when all else was gone'.

Famines were not rare in Ireland: there were perhaps 30 severe episodes between 1300 and 1800, including a disastrous failure of the potato crop in 1740. The sheer size of the population dependent on the potato, however—three million or so—made the arrival, in August 1845, of the potato blight fungus *phytophthora infestans* the worst such event in Irish history. That year, one-third of the crop was rotten and inedible; by 1847, most of the seed potatoes had been eaten by desperate people. In the first year of the famine, the Tory government of Robert Peel responded by importing £100,000 worth of Indian meal from the US and establishing a programme of public works. The Liberal administration of Lord John Russell, which took office in 1846, continued the works programme, but was reluctant to interfere with market forces. A combination of laissez-faire ideology, a 'providential' evangelical theology that

saw the famine as God's way of correcting the vices of the Irish and a severe economic recession in Britain greatly limited the scale and speed of the official response. While some private organisations, notably the Society of Friends (Quakers), made heroic efforts to save lives, the government refused to stop the export of food from Ireland—causing extreme bitterness for decades to come.

In February 1847 ideology and theology were set aside and public kitchens were established, to feed the starving without demanding work in return. In September, however, the government insisted that further relief would be supplied only at already overcrowded and insanitary workhouses. This concentration of sick and starving people undoubtedly created ideal conditions for the spread of the diseases—principally typhus and relapsing fever—that killed more people than hunger alone. Misery was piled on misery; landlords, under pressure from rising taxation and falling rents, evicted tenants at a rate that rose to 100,000 a year by 1850.

Roughly one million people died (proportionally more than in any other known famine) and a similar number emigrated. Patterns of mass migration were reinforced. The decimation of the cottier class changed both the social structure and the prevailing culture—those who died or left were disproportionately Irish-speaking. A new Ireland emerged from the disaster, as Catholic beef farmers took over the vacated land. The famine ended but, in these respects, it has never gone away.

100 WHERE TO SEE IT: NATIONAL MUSEUM OF IRELAND-MUSEUM OF COUNTRY LIFE, TURLOUGH PARK, CASTLEBAR, CO. MAYO; 00-353-94-9031755; WWW.MUSEUM.IE/EN/INTRO/COUNTRY-LIFE.ASPX

This humble object tells two stories of wandering people. It is a tin teapot, with a pouring lip soldered onto one side and the internal wall of the cup punctured with holes to make a strainer. It was made in Tuam, Co. Galway, by an old tinker, Mike Maughan, and collected in 1961. Maughan was responding to a request to make the kind of vessel that his family had traditionally made for nineteenth-century emigrants. Preparing for the long sea voyage to America, and unwilling to do without the tea for which the Irish had acquired an insatiable thirst, emigrants would buy these specially-designed pots. They were made by travelling people in an era before 'tinker' became a term of abuse. The deftness of the object suggests that the Travellers were well attuned to the market for their goods.

It is telling that Irish folk culture developed its own objects specifically for the act of emigration. The sheer scale of outward migration in the decade of the Great Famine is staggering: 2.1 million people. More people left Ireland in the 11 years immediately after the famine than during the previous 250 years. Some left on what Thomas D'Arcy McGee first called 'sailing coffins', and many were ragged, famished and diseased. Many settled permanently in Britain, especially in ports such as Liverpool; around 340,000 went to Canada and 1.5 million to the United States; smaller numbers settled in Australia, New Zealand and South Africa. Even after this first wave of refugee migrants, Irish people continued to leave in droves, impelled not by hunger but by the push of poverty and the pull of urban industrial life. Between 1856 and 1921, between 4.1 and 4.5 million adults and children emigrated (passenger lists show large number of children travelling alone). It is especially striking that, almost uniquely, Irish emigration was as heavily female as male—the Irish maid, and later the Irish public school teacher, were as much stock figures in American life as the Irish navvy or publican.

At one level, these experiences were part of European life: 26 million Europeans left for the New World between 1840 and 1900, and emigration was a significant aspect of life in every country except France. Ireland, however, was an extreme case—in the proportion of the population that emigrated, in the persistence of mass migration, in the number of women who went and in the very low rate of return, even from nearby England. Emigration became, not a response to crisis, but a natural expectation. 'Children', wrote one contemporary observer, 'learn from their childhood that their destiny is America; and as they grow up the thought is set before them as a thing to hope for'. Ironically, the leaving of Ireland became one of the real markers of Irish identity. Leopold Bloom, in James Joyce's *Ulysses*, asked to define a nation, says it is 'the same people living in the same place'. Then remembering that he is Irish (and Jewish), he adds 'or also living in different places'. The remarkable fact was that the Irish, scattered among the continents, did retain some sense of being 'the same people'.

100 WHERE TO SEE IT: NATIONAL MUSEUM OF IRELAND-MUSEUM OF COUNTRY LIFE, TURLOUGH PARK, CASTLEBAR, CO. MAYO; 00-353-94-9031755; WWW.MUSEUM.IE/EN/INTRO/COUNTRY-LIFE.ASPX

This spectacular 125 ounce, 22 carat gold cup is perhaps the first really eloquent object of the Irish diaspora. It was made in Melbourne, Australia, by Irish-born goldsmith William Hackett, using nuggets donated by Irish miners, and presented to an Irish nationalist hero, William Smith O'Brien. It brings together the two sides of Irish emigration—political deportation in the case of O'Brien, who was transported to Van Diemen's Land in July 1849, having been found guilty of high treason; and the ordinary economic migration of those who sought opportunity beyond post-famine Ireland.

Gold was discovered in 1851 and over 100,000 Irish immigrants made their way to Australasia over the next decade. As was the case elsewhere, they had mixed fortunes. In the countryside, some became highly successful farmers, but sympathy for the bush-ranging gang led by Ned Kelly epitomised continuing resentment of the power of large, mostly British, landholders. In Melbourne, Irish-born lawyers, doctors, and other professionals, mostly graduates of Trinity College Dublin, gained positions of status and privilege, while many unskilled Irish migrants struggled to gain a secure foothold.

The Irish émigré community as a whole, though, was enthused by O'Brien's release from Van Diemen's Land in 1854. John O'Shanasy, from Co. Tipperary (later to become Sir John and premier of Victoria), organised ceremonies to welcome him and two other ex-prisoners to Melbourne. At a large public banquet, O'Brien was presented with an illuminated address and a sheet showing the design of the gold cup to be created in his honour. Irish diggers in the gold field of Ballarat presented O'Brien with a gold nugget and later collected the gold with which to make Hackett's design a reality.

Patriotic fervour and resentment at English power were obvious motives for this generosity, but there was also a broader desire for the comfort of a connection with home. In the year after the cup was made, one gold digger, Michael Normile from Co. Clare, wrote in response to a letter from his father at home 'I received your welcome letter…which gave me and my Sister an ocean of consolation'. In the permanence and solidity of gold there was a similar consolation.

Nevertheless, the iconography of the cup suggests how mass emigration was already complicating that story. The top has Hibernia carrying a cap of liberty and crowning O'Brien with a laurel wreath, but the bottom of the main cup is decorated with two interesting kinds of symbols. There are images of ancient gold torcs, lunulae and brooches—along with the now-standard Irish imagery of shamrocks and wolfhounds —showing how notions of antiquity were becoming important to Irish identity. On the sides, in wild incongruity, are a kangaroo and an emu. Already, there is the sense of an Irishness that looks back to a distant time, even while it has to acknowledge its present situation in an even more distant place.

100 WHERE TO SEE IT: NATIONAL MUSEUM OF IRELAND-DECORATIVE ARTS AND HISTORY, COLLINS BARRACKS, BENBURB STREET, DUBLIN 7; 00-353-1-6777444; WWW.MUSEUM.IE

This ornate silver casket, with by now standard imagery of round towers, wolfhounds and 'Celtic' filigrees, and a representation of the former (and hoped-for future) Irish parliament, was presented by 'the nationalists of Drogheda' to Charles Stewart Parnell in 1884. He was then near the summit of his prestige as the 'uncrowned king of Ireland'.

Parnell was an unlikely leader of Irish nationalism. Born into a Protestant landowning family in Avondale, Co. Wicklow, and educated at Cambridge, he was nervous, superstitious and sometimes withdrawn. At his height, however, he was a brilliant political strategist. Within five years of election as Home Rule MP for Co. Meath in 1875, he had established control over the previously fractious Irish parliamentary party at Westminster and the extra-parliamentary Land League. To do so, he had to appeal to respectable middle-class nationalists, militant tenant farmers and physical-force republicans belonging to the Fenian secret society, which staged an abortive 'rising' in 1867. Parnell was a pragmatist who could hint effortlessly at revolutionary intent.

His boldest stroke was to accept the presidency of the Land League, founded in Dublin in 1879 by Fenian gun-runner Michael Davitt. Its long-term demand was for tenants to become owners of the land; in the short-term it focused on the 'three Fs': fair rents, free sale and fixity of tenure. Its tactics became increasingly militant: rent strikes, physical impeding of evictions, mass meetings and, its signature tactic, the boycott, a term coined to describe the organised ostracism of Mayo land agent Captain Hugh Boycott in 1880.

Parnell fused these tactics with an obstructionist campaign at Westminster, to keep the Irish land question near the top of the British political agenda. His triumph was the 1881 Land Act, which granted the three Fs and established a land commission with powers to set rents and make loans to tenants wishing to purchase their holdings. It was the first in a series of acts (1885, 1891 and 1903) that gradually accomplished a momentous social change—the transfer of the vast bulk of Irish land from landlords to peasant proprietors.

After the first land act Parnell shifted his focus to Home Rule—autonomy for Ireland within the empire. When he led 86 Home Rule MPs to Westminster in 1885, gaining the balance of power, he cemented an alliance with Prime Minister William Gladstone. He now had a formidable alliance for Home Rule, from the Catholic bishops to the Liberal Party. In 1886 a Home Rule bill was defeated in the House of Commons, but only by 30 votes.

From this zenith, Parnell's power declined. Poor health and a long-term affair with Katherine O'Shea, wife of one of his more disreputable MPs, diverted his energies. He briefly regained his heroic status in 1890, because of a failed smear campaign linking him to secret support for rural crime. He was then cited by O'Shea's husband in a divorce petition and lost the support of the Catholic bishops. The party split bitterly; Parnell died in Brighton in 1891, aged just 45.

172

WHERE TO SEE IT: NATIONAL MUSEUM OF IRELAND-DECORATIVE ARTS AND HISTORY, COLLINS BARRACKS, BENBURB STREET, DUBLIN 7; 00-353-1-6777444; WWW.MUSEUM.IE

It is extraordinary to think that this dazzlingly lavish, twenty-foot high, pulpit was made for an Irish Catholic church just half a century after the devastation of the Great Hunger. It captures the most remarkable aspect of the second half of the nineteenth century in Ireland: the triumph of a new, highly organised Catholicism that took control of many aspects of life. From the trauma of the famine emerged an institution that defined the identity of the majority of the population for the next 150 years.

The pulpit is of a mediaeval grandeur. It was carved, from the finest oak, by artists in the Belgian city of Bruges and unveiled in the Cathedral of the Assumption in Carlow in October 1899. While the execution may be foreign, there is no doubt that the overall conception of the piece is specifically Irish. The message of the pulpit is that the Irish church is now fully intertwined with European, and therefore Roman, Catholicism. The first panel, just below the balustrade, shows St Patrick preaching to the High King at Tara, with a statue of St Brigid beside it. Other Irish saints, Laserian and Conleth, are represented on further panels. The image of St Paul is based on a Raphael painting in the Vatican and the crucifix on the reredos is based on a painting by Van Dyke in the cathedral in Bruges. Thus, Irish Catholicism is fully fused with the universal church.

There is another message too. An angel at the base holds a scroll that says *Vox Hibernorum*—'the voice of the Irish', an allusion to Patrick but also a reminder of who it is that now speaks for the Irish. Almost all the scenes on the panels are of preaching, and the majesty of the pulpit itself, raising the priest high above the congregation, declares the absolute authority of the preacher's voice.

A massive programme of church building had begun in Ireland even before the famine was over. Churches designed by the great English neo-Gothic architect Augustus Pugin, notably Enniscorthy and Killarney cathedrals, were being built even while millions were starving. Under the leadership of Paul Cullen, who became archbishop of Armagh in 1849 and Ireland's first cardinal in 1866, the church co-operated closely with the state, assumed control of the primary education and health systems (largely through orders such as the Christian Brothers and the Sisters of Mercy, founded by Edmund Rice and Catherine McAuley, respectively), and became highly centralised, authoritarian and dogmatically orthodox. A 'devotional revolution' submerged older, semi-pagan practices that centred on holy wells, patterns and wakes and instead structured religious life around sacraments, sermons, missions led by fiery preachers and confraternities.

In this revolution, the church gained control of the process of modernisation, shaping the ways in which Irish people learned to conform to Victorian standards of comportment, and imposing rigid sexual ideals. It gave a society shamed by a great catastrophe a way to be respectable. In its beautiful new places of worship, the church provided calm, comfort and dignity. For millions of emigrants, its universality guaranteed a crucial element of continuity that helped them live with massive disruption. These benefits came at the cost of obedience, but for most Catholics that seemed a price worth paying.

175

This exquisite needlepoint lace collar, made in Youghal, Co. Cork and exhibited at the Royal Dublin Society in August 1906, epitomises one of the more remarkable achievements of Irish women in the second half of the nineteenth century—the creation from scratch of a world-class craft industry.

In 1847 a nun at the Presentation convent in Youghal, Mary Anne Smith, 'conceived the idea of getting up some kind of industrial occupation amongst the poor children attending the convent school such as would help them to earn a livelihood or, at least, keep them from starving'.

Smith found a piece of antique Italian point lace and was struck by the idea that lace-making was a potentially lucrative activity that needed little in the way of initial capital. She unravelled the Italian lace, worked out its complex patterns and began to teach the techniques to those of her pupils most adept at needlework.

Within five years, the convent had developed a regular lace-making school, and by the turn of the century, with Sr Mary Regis heading the school, up to 70 women and girls were making needlepoint and crochet laces at the Youghal Lace Co-operative, with many others working at home. From Youghal, the craft of needlepoint lace spread to Kenmare and New Ross. (A short-lived school at Tynan, Co. Armagh, was founded around the same time as that in Youghal, and a later school was founded at Inishmacsaint, Co. Fermanagh.)

Youghal needlepoint lace was marked by the Italianate techniques developed by Smith, and evident in this floral collar: flat cotton stitching made with fibre thinner than human hair, motifs surrounded by shell stitches (seven tiny stitches on each loop). But the Youghal women also developed 50 new stitches. They had to combine inventiveness with finesse to compete in a market flooded by machine-made lace. Irish laces were a niche product for the well-to-do, and their attractions were greatly enhanced by the cachet of the Arts and Crafts movement of the nineteenth century.

Irish laces quickly became high fashion, worn by everyone from the Pope to Queen Victoria. In 1886 a large quilt of needlepoint lace made at Kenmare was sold to an American millionairess for the then-staggering sum of £300. The industry spread outwards from the convents, although commercial lace production in Limerick and Carrickmacross had developed at an earlier period; each type of lace-making had its own distinctive style and techniques. Lace design was taught and developed at colleges, notably Cork's Crawford School of Art; Irish designers such as Michael Hayes and Eileen O'Donoghue, from Limerick, helped to create styles that appealed to an international market.

Young women did not make fortunes from these delicate skills—eighteen shillings a week was regarded as top earnings for a diligent lace-maker. Nevertheless, these earnings were highly significant in households with very limited incomes. They gave young women a degree of economic value and independence they would not otherwise have enjoyed. An irony of Irish life was that many young women used their savings from lace-making to buy tickets to America.

100 WHERE TO SEE IT: NATIONAL MUSEUM OF IRELAND-DECORATIVE ARTS AND HISTORY, COLLINS BARRACKS, BENBURB STREET, DUBLIN 7; 00-353-1-6777444; WWW.MUSEUM.IE

This gold medal was presented to a Limerick player, P.J. Corbett, a member of the team that won the first all-Ireland Gaelic football championship final. On 1 November 1884, at Hayes's Hotel in Thurles, Co. Tipperary, Michael Cusack convened the first meeting of the 'Gaelic Athletic Association for the Preservation and Cultivation of National Pastimes'. Cusack had been an enthusiast for rugby and cricket. Another of the prime movers, Maurice Davin, was an accomplished all-round athlete. In the atmosphere of the 1880s, they and others were now determined that Ireland should have its own distinctive sporting culture. The GAA thus set out to take control of Irish athletics, to codify the ancient sport of hurling and to develop Gaelic football, a version of the game influenced by both rugby and soccer. Indeed, in its first two or three years, it was the GAA's athletics events that were its most popular aspect.

In one sense, the GAA was a very 'British' development, part of the great Victorian drive to codify all kinds of games and turn them into popular spectacles. Thus, although it found its greatest support among the growing class of 'strong farmers', the GAA was in many ways a typical product of ninteeenth-century modernisation. All over Europe, a new popular nationalism looked to culture as the basis for a collective identity that could bind together an increasingly literate and mobile population.

In Ireland, these notions had a particular appeal. After the fall of Parnell, the parliamentary Irish party was bitterly split and Home Rule was a more distant prospect. Even prior to the split energy was being channelled into a remarkable ferment of civic activity: Irish language revivalists were active from the late 1870s, and there was also development in relation to the agricultural co-operative movement (by 1914, there were over 800 co-ops on the island), trade unions (the Irish Trade Union Congress was established in 1893) and campaigns for votes for women (the Irish Women's Franchise League was founded in 1908).

Much energy also went into the cultural nationalism of the GAA, the Gaelic League (established in 1893 with the aim of reviving Irish as the vernacular language), pipe bands, Inghinidhe na hÉireann (Daughters of Ireland) and the Irish Literary Theatre. These last two organisations fed into the creation, in 1904, of the Abbey Theatre. Its great early figures, William Butler Yeats, Augusta, Lady Gregory, and John Millington Synge gave international prestige to the idea of a distinctive Irish culture (albeit in the English language).

These attempts at 'cultural revival' were remarkably successful, and whereas interest in all sports, including in rugby and soccer, grew dramatically at this time, by 1915, Gaelic football was the most popular spectator sport on the island and the GAA was well on the way to becoming arguably the most remarkable amateur sporting body in the world.

The Gaelic League never succeeded in making Irish the vernacular, but it did have an enormous influence on younger nationalists. Yet hopes that culture would be a terrain on which political and religious differences could be left behind were disappointed. Politics could not be forgotten—both the GAA and the Gaelic League were heavily infiltrated by the secretive Irish Republican Brotherhood. The football championship for which P.J. Corbett won his medal was begun in 1887, but it was delayed because of fierce political infighting between IRB, clerical and non-aligned supporters within the association, and the final itself was not played until 29 April 1888; in a further twist, the medals were not presented until c. 1912, because of a lack of money within the GAA.

Many Protestants—among them Douglas Hyde, George Russell and the Abbey writers—were key figures in the cultural revival, but it was difficult to escape the identification of 'Irish Ireland' with 'Catholic Ireland'. Hyde's insistence that the Gaelic League should avoid politics led to his resignation as its president in 1915. With nationalism becoming such a powerful force in modern Europe, and looking to culture to support its claims, avoiding politics was perhaps an impossible aspiration.

100 WHERE TO SEE IT: NATIONAL MUSEUM OF IRELAND-DECORATIVE ARTS AND HISTORY, COLLINS BARRACKS, BENBURB STREET, DUBLIN 7; 00-353-1-6777444; WWW.MUSEUM.IE

This seraphically beautiful Buddha, now in the National Museum in Dublin, is a piece of imperial loot. In the Mandalay style, which dates it to 1857–86, the statue is of marble, with the drapery painted gold. It represents the dying but beatific Buddha, preparing for his death and ascent into Nirvana. Colonel Sir Charles Fitzgerald, an Irishman in the British army in India, stole it while on a punitive military expedition to Burma in 1885–6. In 1891, Fitzgerald sent it, along with other looted Burmese statues, to the National Museum.

Audrey Whitty identified the statue as the one which is mentioned twice in perhaps the most important Irish work of literature of the twentieth century, James Joyce's *Ulysses* (set in 1904 and published in 1922). The novel's hero Leopold Bloom thinks of 'Buddha their God lying on his side in the museum, Taking it easy with his hand under his cheek'. Later, Bloom's wife Molly recalls him:

> Breathing with his hand on his nose like that Indian god he took me to show one wet Sunday in the museum in Kildare Street all yellow in a pinafore, lying on his side on his hand with his ten toes sticking out.

Other imperial objects ended up in Ireland. In 1904 the museum purchased for £100, 41 metalwork objects from Lhasa, brought back from the British invasion of Tibet. (The Treaty of Lhasa, opening up Tibet to British trade, was drawn up by an Irishman, Captain Frederick O'Connor, the leading linguist on the Francis Younghusband expedition to Tibet, 1903–04.) They are reminders that Ireland was not only a victim of British imperialism. Very large numbers of Irish people participated in the expansion and maintenance of the empire, most as foot soldiers, but many as high-ranking military and civil administrators, missionaries, doctors and other professionals.

In one of the great literary expressions of the imperial spirit, Rudyard Kipling's *Kim*, the wild-child hero explains that his name is Kim Rishti ke. What, he is asked, is Rishti? 'Eye-rishti—that was the regiment—my father's'. 'Irish, oh I see'. The 'rishti' were indeed common enough to get their own word in the Hindi language. Key figures in the extension and maintenance of British rule in India included Laurence Sullivan from Cork, George Macartney from Antrim (who was also the British envoy who tried, and failed, to open up imperial trade with China), John Nicholson from Dublin, and Sir Michael O'Dwyer, from a Catholic family in Tipperary, who led the suppression of protest in the Punjab between 1913 and 1920. O'Dwyer's religion was not typical but neither was it entirely unusual: by the late-nineteenth century, 30 per cent of Irish recruits to the Indian civil service were Catholic.

Irish involvement in the empire reached its height with the Boer War in South Africa between 1899 and 1902. A few hundred Irish nationalists fought for the Boers, and leading militants at home—including W.B. Yeats, Maud Gonne, James Connolly and Arthur Griffith—campaigned in their favour. Nevertheless, 28,000 Irishmen fought for the British in South Africa. Anti-imperialism was becoming more vigorous, but it was still a minority position.

100 WHERE TO SEE IT: NATIONAL MUSEUM OF IRELAND-DECORATIVE ARTS AND HISTORY, COLLINS BARRACKS, BENBURB STREET, DUBLIN 7; 00-353-1-6777444; WWW.MUSEUM.IE

Launch

OF

White Star Royal Mail Triple-Screw Steamer

"TITANIC"

At BELFAST,

Wednesday, 31st May, 1911, at 12-15 p.m.

Admit Bearer.

Shortly after noon on 31 May 1911, a huge crowd gathered at the Harland and Wolff (H&W) shipyard at Queen's Island in Belfast Lough for the launch of the great transatlantic liner, *Titanic*. Among them were many of the workers who had built her. This admission ticket belonged to David Moneypenny, a ship's painter who worked on the first-class quarters. For him, for his colleagues, for Belfast and for Protestant Ulster, this was a moment of extraordinary accomplishment. *Titanic* was at the leading edge of twentieth-century technology.

That such a world-beating ship was created in an Irish city was astonishing, but then Belfast was a new kind of Irish place. It had grown at a phenomenal rate, surging past Dublin in 1891 to become Ireland's largest city, and growing by another 35 per cent over the rest of that decade.

Titanic was built on an existing foundation of industrial and technological superlatives: in 1899 H&W had launched the world's largest ship, the *Oceanic*. Belfast also had, as Jonathan Bardon notes, the world's 'largest rope works, tobacco factory, linen spinning mill, tea machinery works, dry dock and aerated water factory'. There was no chance that southern Ireland, lacking this kind of globally significant industry, could have produced *Titanic*—it belonged to an imperial and industrial world. Its creators were largely Protestant—2000 Catholics worked in the shipyard but they were not part of its official story: the ship was universally hailed as a 'great Anglo-Saxon triumph'.

With the industrial north-east so deeply integrated into an imperial economy, it was never

likely that the idea of a Home Rule Ireland, dominated by agricultural interests and heavily influenced by the Catholic church, would be easily sold to the Protestants who built *Titanic*. Indeed, *Titanic* herself came to be represented in popular culture through two quite different versions of Ireland. One was the steerage-class emigrants among the 1500 who drowned on the early morning of 15 April 1912 when the great ship sank on her maiden voyage. The other was an Ulster Protestant identity, in which that tragedy seemed to foretell a wider doom, an almost apocalyptic sense of threat. Three days after *Titanic* sank, the third Home Rule Bill was introduced into the House of Commons in London. Three months later, vicious and organised assaults forced all Catholics out of the shipyards.

On 28 September, 237,000 men and 234,000 women, from all classes of Protestant Ireland, signed the Ulster Covenant or an associated declaration, committing the men to 'using all means which may be found necessary to defeat the present conspiracy to set up a Home Rule Parliament in Ireland'. In January 1913, the Ulster Unionist Council, under Dublin-born Edward Carson, decided to organise 100,000 signatories of the covenant into an Ulster Volunteer Force and to train them in the use of firearms. These events created two paradoxes: a violent loyalist rebellion against the state to which it pledged its allegiance, and an Irish nationalism appealing to the idea of a unified nation whose existence was anything but obvious.

WHERE TO SEE IT: NATIONAL MUSEUMS NORTHERN IRELAND-ULSTER FOLK AND TRANSPORT MUSEUM, CULTRA, HOLYWOOD, CO. DOWN BT18 0EU; 00-44-845-6080000; WWW.NMNI.COM/UFTM

This lamp is from a converted collier, the *River Clyde*. On 25 April 1915 it lit the way to hell for 2000 soldiers, mostly members of the Munster and Dublin Fusiliers. They had been chosen as the shock troops of an Allied landing near Sedd-el-Bahr at Cape Helles, on the southern tip of the Gallipoli peninsula in Turkey. The Gallipoli operation was intended to break the military stalemate on the western front that had developed since the outbreak of the First World War—the monumental clash of great European empires that began in August 1914 and quickly earned its name as the Great War.

The *River Clyde* was deliberately run aground beneath an old fortress, while most of the Dubliners tried to get ashore in open boats. Both regiments made perfect targets for the Turkish gunners in the fort. One officer recalled that the men on the open boats were 'literally slaughtered like rats in a trap'. Another recalled that the landing as he experienced it:

> was pure butchery and we were at the receiving end. They called it a 'landing' but it was hardly even that at the beginning. The dear men were just mown down in scores into a bloody silence as they showed themselves at the *Clyde's* open hatches.

The Dublins had 25 officers and 987 other ranks but only one officer and 374 others made it ashore, many of them wounded. Among the Munsters, about 600 were killed or wounded. The scale of the casualties was such that the battalions were temporarily amalgamated into a single unit, known as the Dubsters.

It would have been hard to remember, at that point, that the outbreak of the war was greeted by many in Ireland with some relief. Ireland had been on the brink of civil war over Home Rule, but the infinitely larger conflict superseded this insular row. Although Home Rule was finally passed in September 1914, its implementation was immediately postponed for the duration of the war. The Nationalist leader John Redmond supported the war effort. Over 200,000 Irishmen fought in the war. Optimists dared to hope that the experience of fighting side-by-side in a relatively short and triumphant campaign would create a new sympathy between Ulster Protestants and southern Catholics.

Optimism, not just for Ireland but for humanity, was bled dry on the beaches of Gallipoli and in the mud of France and Belgium. On 1 July 1916, the 36th (Ulster) Division was in the forefront of the offensive on the Somme, suffering 5500 casualties, including 2000 dead—a catastrophe seared into the collective consciousness of Protestant Ulster. The 16th (Irish) Division lost 4330 men (1200 dead) in the same battle in September. At Messines Ridge in June 1917 the two divisions went into battle together—among the dead was Redmond's brother Willie. In all, at least 35,000 Irishmen died. The war did form a common experience for Irishmen of different traditions, but it was the experience of a scarcely imaginable cataclysm.

WHERE TO SEE IT: NATIONAL MUSEUM OF IRELAND-DECORATIVE ARTS AND HISTORY, COLLINS BARRACKS, BENBURB STREET, DUBLIN 7; 00-353-1-6777444; WWW.MUSEUM.IE; ON LOAN FROM NATIONAL ARMY MUSEUM, ROYAL HOSPITAL ROAD, CHELSEA, LONDON SW3 4HT; 00-44-20-7730-0717; WWW.NAM.AC.UK

This undershirt was worn by James Connolly in the General Post Office in Dublin during Easter Week 1916. The blood is from a flesh wound on his upper arm; he was far more severely wounded in the leg and had to be strapped to a chair at his execution by firing squad for his role in the abortive Rising. Connolly, born in Edinburgh of Irish parents, was a key figure in the ferment of radical agitation that preceded the rebellion. He was an organiser for the Irish Transport and General Workers' Union (ITGWU) and helped found the Labour Party in 1912. He was imprisoned during the Lockout in 1913, when Dublin's employers shut out workers who would not give up membership of the ITGWU.

Able and charismatic as he was, Connolly might have remained a marginal figure. The Irish parliamentary party, reunited under John Redmond, remained the dominant force in nationalist politics. The Great War, however, changed everything. Redmond's support for the war left a space for revolutionary nationalism to occupy. A small breakaway group from the Irish Volunteers came under the control of the Irish Republican Brotherhood, which secretly planned a rising for which it hoped to have German support. Connolly, with his tiny Citizen Army, did likewise. In the event just 1200 rebels, with no effective German aid, occupied public buildings in Dublin for six days in April 1916.

The main casualties were civilians, 230 were killed, compared with 132 soldiers or policemen and 64 rebels. Yet the official response to the insurrection—execution of fifteen rebel leaders and mass arrests of nationalists—helped turn the dead rebels into martyrs. In the 1918 general election Redmond faced a resurgent Sinn Féin, a reconstitution of a small, non-violent nationalist party that had been mistakenly blamed for the Rising. Sinn Féin took less than half the vote but won 73 of the 105 Irish seats at parliament. Its MPs then seceded from Westminster and established the first Dáil, which met in Dublin in January 1919, declaring an independent Irish republic.

The Dáil, however, was increasingly pushed aside by what was by then known as the Irish Republican Army, which later that month shot dead two policemen in Tipperary. The conflict that began with these shootings continued, with the IRA using guerrilla tactics and the London government sending in irregular units—the Black and Tans and Auxiliaries, whose often atrocious behaviour further alienated much of the population—until a truce was declared in July 1921. In the meantime, the Government of Ireland Act of 1920 had established a six-county Northern Ireland. A treaty signed on 21 December 1921 established the twenty-six county Free State as a self-governing entity within the British Commonwealth.

The treaty was supported by Michael Collins and Arthur Griffith but opposed by Éamon de Valera; it was ratified by the Dáil in January 1922 by 64 votes to 57. The defeated minority revolted, leading to a short but bloody Civil War. It was not the birth that Connolly and his comrades had imagined for an Irish state, but most of Ireland did, at last, have an independent government.

WHERE TO SEE IT: NATIONAL MUSEUM OF IRELAND-DECORATIVE ARTS AND HISTORY, COLLINS BARRACKS, BENBURB STREET, DUBLIN 7; 00-353-1-6777444; WWW.MUSEUM.IE

In January 1926 Minister for Finance Ernest Blythe told the Dáil that the new Irish Free State should have 'a coinage distinctively our own, bearing the devices of this country'. A committee, chaired by the poet and senator W.B. Yeats, was asked to adjudicate on the best designs submitted. One was by sculptor Jerome Connor. Born in Annascaul, Co. Kerry, he emigrated to Massachusetts when he was fourteen and eventually established his own studio in Washington, DC. He moved back to Ireland in 1925 to work on a memorial to those who lost their lives in the sinking of the *Lusitania* off the Cork coast in 1915.

This is Connor's 1927 proposal for the penny coin. He thought of the penny as a child's coin and conceived a design that celebrated childhood—the scampish boy is based on his own grand-nephew John.

It was, on the face of it, an image appropriate to the new state's aspirations. The Democratic Programme adopted by the first Dáil in 1919 had set itself a very high aim:

> It shall be the first duty of the Government of the Republic to make provision for the physical, mental and spiritual well-being of the children, to secure that no child shall suffer hunger or cold from lack of food, clothing, or shelter.

Many children in the new Ireland did enjoy a safe and happy upbringing, but the aspiration to ensure that no child went hungry or cold was certainly not met. Moreover, children were among the worst victims of the dark side of the new state: its elaborate system of social repression through which 'problem' citizens were incarcerated in harsh, sometimes dangerous institutions.

Between the 1920s and the 1950s, more than one per cent of the population was locked up in a mental hospital, a Magdalene laundry, where women thought to be at risk of sexual immorality were made to work without pay, or an industrial school. To these latter institutions, run by religious orders, one child in every hundred was sent. Between 1936 and 1970 approximately 170,000 children entered the gates of one or other of the 50 or so industrial schools, staying on average for seven years. The great majority were committed, not because they were guilty of any offence, but because their families were deemed to be 'needy'.

A commission of inquiry established in 2000 found that severe beatings were pervasive in both boys' and girls' schools and that, in the institutions for boys, sexual abuse was 'endemic'. The commission also found that such abuse was allowed to continue because of a general 'culture of silence' and because of the 'deferential and submissive attitude' of the state authorities towards the religious congregations.

This was the cruel side of what many in the new state would have regarded as its greatest virtues—its strong emphasis on sexual morality and social control and reverence for religious institutions. For some, those virtues were a source of great pride. For others, they were the excuse for a systematic abuse of power over society's most vulnerable members.

100 WHERE TO SEE IT: NATIONAL MUSEUM OF IRELAND-DECORATIVE ARTS AND HISTORY, COLLINS BARRACKS, BENBURB STREET, DUBLIN 7; 00-353-1-6777444; WWW.MUSEUM.IE

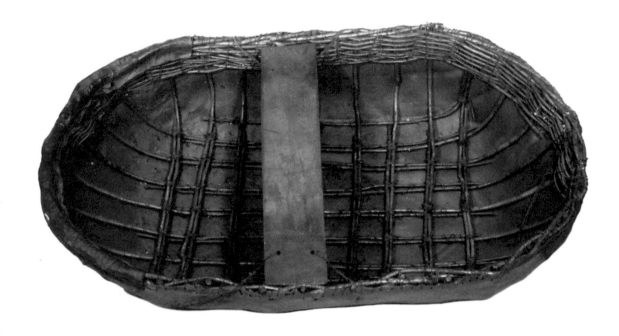

When people first came to Ireland around 10,000 years ago, almost certainly they were familiar with skin boat technology. There are images of coracles (or curachs as they have long been known in Ireland) on stone panels at Nineveh in Iraq from around 700 BC. Mediaeval Irish sources describe St Colmcille going into exile and St Brendan going on a fabulous sea voyage in similar hide-clad boats.

When Michael O'Brien made coracles for salmon fishing on the River Boyne at Oldbridge, Co. Meath in 1928, he was therefore carrying on an immemorial tradition. Its basket-like wooden structure, tightly sealed in leather, harks all the way back to the island's first inhabitants. The Boyne coracles were oval shaped, generally made from woven hazel rods and covered with locally tanned cow-hides; the size varied from six feet by four feet to six-and-a-half feet by four feet, so that the vessels could easily be covered using a single, large hide.

Ireland had been, over the previous century, a place of traumatic upheaval: land wars, famine, mass emigration, the emergence of industrial Ulster, the shift from Irish to English as the vernacular language. Yet it also retained elements of an extraordinary continuity. The new Irish state tended to exaggerate that continuity, romanticising life in isolated communities, especially on the Aran and Blasket islands off the west coast, as the essential repository of authentic Irishness. The subtle and complex accounts of their own lives given by islanders like Peig Sayers and Tomás Ó Criomhthain were pasteurised into official texts for the state's main cultural project: the revival of the Irish language as the national vernacular. Robert Flaherty's 1934 film, *Man of Aran*, added a layer of timeless myth—not least to the curach itself, which featured centrally in its dramatic scenes of islanders battling against the sea.

Much of the reality—especially poverty and emigration—was winnowed out of this ideal of a noble and ancient culture. (The ironies came home in 1953 when the Blaskets were evacuated and most of the islanders went to live in Springfield, Massachusetts.) The attempt to revive Irish as the everyday language—perhaps always doomed in a society where one in two people would emigrate—failed. Some official policies, such as censorious attempts to stamp out traditions of holding dances in houses and at crossroads, actually damaged the real folk culture.

Yet there was something genuinely remarkable about the degree to which aspects of an older culture really did retain their vigour. The Irish language outlived predictions of death. Traditions of oral storytelling, exemplified by Sayers and recorded by the Irish Folklore Commission, persisted at least into the era of television. Irish music in its different forms, from dance tunes to slow airs to the distinctive, haunting tones of *sean nós* singing, continued to sound out—not just in Ireland but in Irish communities abroad. Ancient religious practices, centred on holy wells and holy mountains, carried on, albeit in Christianised forms.

None of these forms was static—no living culture ever is. Each was open to periodic 'revivals' which were in fact re-inventions. What mattered is that they survived even the potentially stultifying embrace of officialdom. They did so because people still had a use for them and could adapt them to their own times. Curachs are still widely used in the west of Ireland, most of them now covered with fibreglass while retaining their traditional shape. Like so much of Irish culture, they are the same only different.

 WHERE TO SEE IT: NATIONAL MUSEUM OF IRELAND-COUNTRY LIFE, TURLOUGH PARK, CASTLEBAR, CO. MAYO; 00-353-94-9031755; WWW.MUSEUM.IE/EN/INTRO/COUNTRYLIFE.ASPX

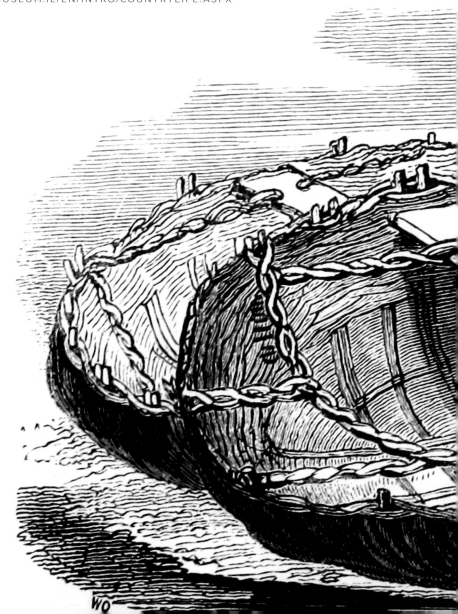

'An armrest was omitted in order to leave the body more freedom in movement and to allow it to bend forward or to turn to the other side unrestricted'. So said Eileen Gray of what she called her 'nonconformist chair'. Or, as Zeev Arum, the furniture dealer who revived many of Gray's startling designs in the 1970s, put it 'you don't need to sit like an emperor to be comfortable'. The chair contains many of the notions at the heart of the Modernist movement in Europe: freedom, individuality, the belief that the form of an object should be determined by its function, the use of industrial materials like tubular steel and aluminium. That its creator was one of the movement's pioneers yet virtually unknown in her native country for most of her life says a great deal about Ireland's ambiguous relationship to European modernity.

Eileen Gray was born in 1878 at Brownswood, near Enniscorthy, Co. Wexford. She studied painting at the Slade School of Art and then in Paris, where she became interested in particular in Japanese lacquer work. In 1917, Gray was commissioned to design the interior of an apartment on Rue de Lota in Paris. She created strikingly innovative objects, including a boat-shaped 'pirogue' sofa and the voluptuous leather and tubular steel 'bibendum' chair that became a much-reproduced twentieth-century design classic. The Romanian-born architecture critic Jean Badovici wrote that 'Eileen Gray occupies the centre of the modern movement. She knows that our time, with its new possibilities of living, necessitates new ways of feeling'. Badovici and Gray collaborated on a stark Modernist house, called E-1027, at Roquebrune near Monaco. She also designed the furniture, including the small, circular, adjustable E-1027 table that is also endlessly copied.

Gray was far from the only Irish artist at the cutting edge of cultural innovation in Europe. Her contemporary in Paris, James Joyce, was a leading figure of literary Modernism. Yet independent Ireland as a whole struggled to assert a place in the invention of a new European identity. Isolation from the turmoil of contemporary Europe, a tendency to locate national identity only in the rural past, the lack of a dynamic industrial base, a strong relationship with the United States and state censorship all contributed to the failure to develop a strong European identity. It was not until the late 1950s that tentative official efforts to rethink the relationship with Europe began; even then the idea of joining the then six-member European Economic Community was largely shaped by the reality that Britain was attempting to do so.

As it happened, the process was tortuous: Ireland eventually joined on 1 January 1973. Initially, for most of those who voted in a referendum to join the EEC, the main attraction was undoubtedly economic. It took many years before it became clear that Europe might also provide an imaginative space in which the claustrophobic conundrums of Irish (and British) identity might be re-envisaged. The embrace of Eileen Gray as an important Irish artist was a tiny but telling aspect of that shift. The Irish state acquired Gray's personal collection and her archive on behalf of the Irish people in 2002; it was brought back to Ireland through the efforts of Pat Wallace, former director of the National Museum, and the minister at the time, Síle de Valera.

198

WHERE TO SEE IT: NATIONAL MUSEUM OF IRELAND-DECORATIVE ARTS AND HISTORY, COLLINS BARRACKS, BENBURB STREET, DUBLIN 7; 00-353-1-6777444; WWW.MUSEUM.IE

In the 1950s, a popular Irish song was Sigerson Clifford's gently nostalgic ballad, 'The boys of Barr na Sráide'. It recalls the author's childhood friends in the Kerry town of Cahirsiveen and praises them as the 'men who beat the Black and Tan'. Then, almost as a matter of course, it mentions that they are now scattered: 'And now they toil on foreign soil, for they have gone their way / Deep in the heart of London town or over in Broadway'.

Emigration was one feature of Irish life largely unchanged by partition and independence. (Some of it was directly related to political turmoil: the Protestant population of the 26 counties declined by one-third between 1911 and 1926 and significant numbers of Catholics north of the border were displaced by violent attacks.) The Great Depression that began in 1929 limited the numbers going to the US; Britain, ironically, became the primary destination. The Second World War gave a large boost to migration to Britain—about 120,000 people from the island of Ireland joined the British armed forces; roughly 60,000 of those were from the south. Another 170,000 went from the south to take up jobs in the war economy. It was expected—and, by government ministers, feared—that many of these would return after the war.

Instead, more migrants left for Britain and elsewhere. Three out of every five of those who came of age in Ireland in the 1950s emigrated. Young men, typically with little more than primary education, left to work on building sites (plentiful during post-war reconstruction) and factories

Women worked in factories too, but they were also drawn by the possibilities of higher-status jobs as nurses, teachers and civil service clerks. The suitcase, often a shabby cardboard box with handles, was the most resonant Irish object of the time.

In spite of very high rates of fertility (helped by the banning of artificial contraceptives), the population of the 26 counties declined to a low of 2.8 million and Ireland was left with the lowest known marriage rate in Europe. One contemporary study, *The vanishing Irish*, claimed that 'if this ominous trend continues, in another century, the Irish race will have vanished, much like the Mayans, leaving only their monuments behind them'.

It was impossible to avoid the sense that independent Ireland had failed. Its agricultural economy—largely characterised by small farms and labour-unintensive beef production—could not hold young people increasingly aware of the opportunities offered by urban, industrial life. A policy of protectionism was supposed to create thriving Irish industries but failed to do so. Mass emigration thus raised fundamental questions about the long-term viability of Ireland's hard-won independence. If the break with Britain was not to be written off as a failed experiment, something had to change. In 1958, a white paper called 'Programme for economic expansion', written by the secretary of the Department of Finance, Kenneth Whitaker, called for the end of protectionism and the opening up of Ireland to foreign multinational investment. It would transform, not just economics, but every aspect of Irish life.

201

WHERE TO SEE IT: NATIONAL MUSEUM OF IRELAND-COUNTRY LIFE, TURLOUGH PARK, CASTLEBAR, CO. MAYO; 00-353-94-9031755; WWW.MUSEUM.IE/EN/INTRO/COUNTRY-LIFE.ASPX

The wringer on top of this washing machine makes it look laborious to use, but in the 1950s the manufacturers, Servis, advertised it with slogans like 'a wringer so easy, a child can wring a blanket'. The placing of the upright tub inside a sleek, white cabinet was, at the time, the height of domestic modernity. In an Irish country kitchen, this British-made appliance was an object from a brave new world.

In a roundtable discussion on Irish feminism in 2010, journalist Geraldine Kennedy asked a group of women 'What invention changed any of your lives most?' Mamo McDonald, born in 1929 and long a leading figure in the Irish Countrywomen's Association, replied without hesitation 'the washing machine'. Washing machines had been available to wealthy households in Ireland since the mid-nineteenth century. By the 1940s electric machines were reasonably common in the more prosperous parts of urban Ireland, though still described as 'luxuries'. The really large-scale social impact of the washing machine had to await not just the availability of cheaper automatic machines after the Second World War, but general access to both piped water and electricity in Ireland's still largely rural society.

McDonald recalled that the ICA 'carried out a campaign for water in the home and urged rural women not to marry a farmer unless he installed water in his house as well as his byre…"why would you be bothered putting it into the kitchen, wasn't she well fit to carry a few buckets", [was the] sort of attitude'. The other necessity for washing machines in the home was electricity. In 1925 there were 161 separate local electricity systems in Ireland; these were subsumed into the new state-owned Electricity Supply Board in 1927. The success of the ESB, embodied in the pioneering hydro-electric scheme at Ardnacrusha on the Shannon river, led to the connection of 240,000 consumers by 1945. The huge post-war electrification scheme to connect to the system the 400,000 rural homes still without power was one of the great achievements of independent Ireland.

Peter Sheridan, in his memoir *44: Dublin made me*, recalled the arrival of the washing machine in his working-class home: 'It's a dream machine…the housewife's friend and more reliable than a husband'. The machine liberated women from the time-consuming, back-breaking drudgery of washing clothes (and nappies) by hand.

Organised feminism, from the early 1970s, challenged the idea that a woman's role was confined to the home. In the long term, the contraceptive pill, though only fully legalised in Ireland in 1993, may have had a more revolutionary effect, but the easing of the domestic burden wrought by the arrival of the washing machine was an important prelude to more high-profile changes in the status of women: the lifting (in 1973) of the 'marriage bar' that forced women to leave public service jobs when they married; the right to sit on juries (1976); the right to a share in the family home (1976) and equal pay (1974). There was, by the end of the 1970s, even the hope that washing machines might also be of interest to men.

WHERE TO SEE IT: IRISH AGRICULTURAL MUSEUM, JOHNSTOWN CASTLE ESTATE, CO. WEXFORD; 00-353-53-9184671; WWW.IRISHAGRIMUSEUM.IE

The simple, white handkerchief is distinguished only by the small letters spelling out 'Fr Daly', sewn into it by the mother of its owner, a Catholic priest in Derry. On 30 January 1972, Edward Daly waved it as a plea for a ceasefire, while a group of men tried to carry a seventeen-year-old boy to safety. Jackie Duddy had been shot from behind as he fled from British army paratroopers, who fired on a demonstration organised by the Northern Ireland Civil Rights Association (NICRA). He was one of thirteen unarmed men shot dead that day—seventeen others were wounded and one subsequently died. Images of the harrowing scene made Fr Daly's white handkerchief perhaps the most emblematic object of a thirty-year-long conflict.

On the face of it, the semi-autonomous entity of Northern Ireland was surprisingly successful. Utterly dominated by the Unionist Party, it survived bitter nationalist opposition to partition and the vicious sectarian conflict that raged at its birth. When Taoiseach Seán Lemass travelled to Belfast in 1965 to meet his northern counterpart, Prime Minister Terence O'Neill, it seemed as if Northern Ireland's legitimacy was secure.

Beneath this veneer of stability, however, was a profound problem: one-third of the population was Catholic and suffered discrimination in public employment, the allocation of public housing, the operation of the electoral system and through the activities of the wholly Protestant Ulster Special Constabulary. O'Neill's efforts at reforms after 1963 were thwarted by a backlash led by militant Free Presbyterian preacher Ian Paisley. Catholic expectations had been raised and then dashed; NICRA was formed in 1967. Unionist leaders insisted that NICRA was merely a front for the (in reality moribund) Irish Republican Army and its determination to destroy Northern Ireland.

Conflict escalated: police and loyalist attacks on NICRA marches; sustained riots, especially in Derry; inter-communal violence along sectarian faultlines; the British government's decision of August 1969 to send in troops to keep order; the emergence of a militant, new ('Provisional') IRA and of loyalist paramilitaries; and the disastrous introduction of internment without trial in August 1971. It scarcely mattered that NICRA's initial demands were conceded—after Bloody Sunday, Catholic alienation and Protestant reaction were reinforced by each new atrocity.

Of these, there was no shortage: the death toll rose from 26 in 1970 to 480 in 1972. Attempts to end the violence, most notably the Sunningdale Agreement of 1973 that led to a sharing of power between unionist and nationalist parties, failed. The conflict settled down into an apparently acceptable level of obscenity: 3529 people had died by 2001. Most—around 1800—were civilians. Nationalist paramilitaries killed over 2000; loyalist paramilitaries over 1000, and state security forces over 360. It took a long time before the plea for a truce contained in Fr Daly's improvised white flag was heeded.

205

WHERE TO SEE IT: MUSEUM OF FREE DERRY, BLOODY SUNDAY CENTRE, 55 GLENFADA PARK, DERRY BT48 9DR; 00-44-48-71360880; WWW.MUSEUMOFFREEDERRY.ORG

98. INTEL MICROPROCESSOR, 1994

In 1989 an American microprocessor manufacturer, Intel, opened a factory on a former stud farm in Leixlip, Co. Kildare. It was not an especially sophisticated operation—essentially an assembly line for the basic 486 processor; but the success of that factory led Intel to take a huge gamble on Ireland. It decided to build on the Leixlip campus a facility called Fab 10—the world's first high-volume, 200 millimetre semiconductor wafer plant.

In 1994, when Intel launched the Pentium processor that was central to the emergence of the personal computer as an everyday consumer product, more than half of worldwide processor production was based at Leixlip. Over the next decade, the Irish plant produced one billion Pentium chips. Intel went on to invest over €6 billion at the site, making it the most technologically advanced industrial location in Europe.

Such a development was unimaginable in the 1950s—and not simply because no one predicted the rise of information technology. Ireland was a declining economic backwater, with little sophisticated industry, few global trade links and a poorly educated workforce. The road to Fab 10 began with Ken Whitaker's previously mentioned 'Programme for economic expansion', written in 1958. It was a catalyst for changes that by then were already under way—a shift from economic protectionism to an attempt to attract foreign investment through low corporate taxes. It also provided cover for a major policy shift by the dominant Fianna Fáil party, whose leader Seán Lemass backed Whitaker's strategy.

Change was gradual and, for a long time, seemed likely to shore up rather than threaten established institutions. Nevertheless, the economic boom of the 1960s prepared the ground for a relatively smooth transition to membership of the European Union in 1973.

The belated introduction of free secondary education in 1968 began the formation of a more skilled workforce. Most importantly, Ireland ceased to be a primarily rural society.

Ireland's adjustment to globalisation was by no means easy. The process ran into severe trouble in the 1980s: new jobs failed to keep pace with a burgeoning population and the decline in older industries in the face of international competition. US-led investment took off again in the mid-1990s, however, just as Intel was launching the Pentium. Ireland became the number one location worldwide for US information technology companies and number three for chemicals—exemplified by Pfizer's decision to manufacture its hugely successful Viagra drug exclusively in Ireland. Such investment brought energy, prestige and optimism. As Ireland moved into the twenty-first century, its long history of conflict, emigration and poverty seemed, at last, to be over.

206

On 20 April 2011 a small crowd gathered at St Stephen's Green in Dublin to watch this sign being taken down outside the headquarters of Anglo Irish Bank. They gave a 'small cheer' as it was dismantled. When the sign had been erected over a decade earlier, its design drew on iconic objects of Ireland's past:

> Based on early Irish references such as flint arrowheads, typography from the Book of Kells and crafted gold artefacts, the simplicity of the image sets the tone for a more cohesive corporate identity programme and spearheads measurable improvement in brand awareness.

By the time the sign was removed, Anglo Irish had certainly achieved a very high level of brand awareness—as one of the most notorious banks in world history. It was founded in 1964, but by 1987, its first full year as a publicly quoted company, it had loans of just £92 million and profits of just £1.45 million. At its height in 2007 Anglo was theoretically valued at over €10 billion; its annual profits hit €1.2 billion. Most of that growth was concentrated in the first seven years of the twenty-first century, during which its share price rose by 2000 per cent. Over 80 per cent of its loans—it lent a staggering €18 billion in 2007— were related to property. The bank epitomised the vast Irish property bubble that burst with ruinous consequences in 2008.

The Irish economy had begun to grow rapidly from 1995. The expansion of world trade following the collapse of the Soviet Union and the opening up of China; the boom in information technology; a young and increasingly well-educated population; favourable tax rates that continued to attract multinational corporations; and social changes creating a huge increase in the number of women in the workforce—all were factors in a surge of prosperity.

The value of Irish exports more than doubled between 1995 and 2000. Unemployment halved in the course of the decade, while Gross Domestic Product per head of population rose from three-quarters of the European Union average to 111 per cent. Mass emigration was replaced by a remarkable wave of inward migration from central and eastern Europe, Africa and elsewhere. Ireland became the great success story of economic globalisation.

In reality, the real Irish boom had ended by 2003 and was replaced by a frenzy of investment in property. Ireland's membership of Europe's new currency, the euro, which came into circulation on 1 January 2002, made credit cheap and easily available. This credit, most of which came ultimately from banks in Germany, France and Britain, was mainly spent on property: bank lending for construction increased between 1999 and 2007 from €5.5 billion to €96.2 billion. When the house of cards collapsed in 2008, Anglo was nationalised and eventually wound up, leaving Irish citizens with a bill of around €29 billion and an expensive lesson in the need to remember history.

209

It is a mass-manufactured, international commodity, as iconic in its own dark way as a Coca Cola bottle or an iPhone. Designed by self-taught Russian inventor Mikhail Kalashnikov, the Avtomat Kalashnikova-47, AK47 for short, went into production in 1947. Durable, reliable, adaptable and light, it was exported in huge numbers, initially to the armies of states friendly to the Soviet Union. Its low cost and ease of use, however, gradually made it the weapon of choice for guerrillas, militias and indeed criminal gangs.

The Provisional IRA made extensive use of AK47s, many of them supplied by Libyan leader Muammar Gadaffi in the 1980s, during the conflict in Northern Ireland. So-called Republican paramilitaries caused the majority (58 per cent) of the more than 3,600 deaths in the conflict, including those of 713 innocent civilians. The largest single category of victims, however, was innocent Catholic civilians killed by Loyalist paramilitaries.

By the 1980s, the point of all of this suffering was increasingly unclear. The IRA could not be defeated by military means, but neither could it gain a united Ireland by force. The conflict settled down into an apparently endless series of tit-for-tat killings, punctuated by larger atrocities. As British prime minister Tony Blair put it in 2006, 'No one was ever going to win'.

There were large shifts in the wider context of the Troubles: the collapse of the Soviet Union and the end of the Cold War, the increasingly pluralist nature of Southern Ireland, the effects of Ireland and Britain's common membership of the European Union. Nevertheless, for a long time, the conflict seemed impervious even to these momentous changes. Slowly, however, new possibilities opened up. The IRA's ally Sinn Féin, under the leadership of Gerry Adams and Martin McGuinness, began to see the potential for democratic political organisation. The British government made it clear in 1990 that it had no selfish 'strategic or economic interest' in retaining control of Northern Ireland. Irish governments, largely driven on by the Northern nationalist leader John Hume, stepped up their engagement in the search for a settlement. United States president Bill Clinton took a benign and active interest in the problem.

The tortuous peace process that led to IRA ceasefires in 1994 and 1996 and culminated in the historic Belfast Agreement of 1998, was bedevilled by the issue of IRA arms. Both governments insisted that the IRA should surrender its arsenal. When this proved impossible, a new word gained currency—decommissioning, the putting of weapons 'beyond use'. In September 2005 the IRA finally decommissioned its weapons, laying the ground for a deal that had seemed utterly impossible—the sharing of power between Sinn Féin and the previously hardline Democratic Unionist Party. Most observers accepted that the decommissioning of mutually hostile mindsets would take a great deal longer, but, for once at least, courage, ingenuity and a refusal to accept the apparently inevitable seemed to be on the winning side of Irish history.

WHERE TO SEE IT: NATIONAL MUSEUM OF IRELAND-DECORATIVE ARTS AND HISTORY, COLLINS BARRACKS, BENBURB STREET, DUBLIN 7; 00-353-1-6777444; WWW.MUSEUM.IE

ACKNOWLEDGEMENTS

In some ways, I have my father Samuel to thank for this book. He often brought me and my brothers and sisters to the National Museum in Kildare Street, giving me a great fondness for that wonderful national institution. That esteem has been enormously enhanced in the course of working on this project.

From the beginning, the idea of 'A History of Ireland in 100 Objects' was a collaboration between *The Irish Times* and the National Museum. It would not have even begun without the enthusiastic support and sound advice of the museum's then director, Dr Pat Wallace. His commitment to the principle that the museum's treasures are the common possession of the Irish people, and indeed of humanity as a whole, has been a guiding spirit of this whole enterprise. I am deeply grateful for his generosity and for the practical help and courtesy of Aoife McBride, secretary to the museum's board.

Even that would have been insufficient, however, without the equally open and helpful attitude of the museum's curators, who gave freely of their time and knowledge. Raghnall Ó Floinn and Lar Joye have had a particularly significant involvement in bringing the project to a conclusion. The luminous photographs by Valerie Dowling, Bryan Rutledge and Peter Moloney, with assistance from Anne Keenan, constitute at least half of the value of this whole project. Directors and curators of other museums and institutions were also immediately willing to help, showing a spirit of public service that should be acknowledged more often than it is.

I should stress, however, that the ultimate selection of the objects for the project is my own, as are any errors of fact or eccentricities of interpretation.

I would like in particular to thank the following people for direct assistance with specific objects or other aspects of the project:

Mike Aynsley, Group Chief Executive, Irish Bank Resolution Corporation Limited
Anita Barrett, Cataloguer, County Museum Dundalk
William Blair, Head of Human History, National Museums Northern Ireland
Mary Broderick, Curator, Ephemera Collection, National Library of Ireland
Mary Cahill, Assistant Keeper, Irish Antiquities Division, National Museum of Ireland
Brendan J. Cannon, Corporate Affairs Manager, Intel Ireland
Adrian Corcoran, Office of Public Works Manager, Derrynane House
Catriona Crowe, Head of Special Projects, National Archives of Ireland
Pauric Dempsey, Head of Communications and Public Affairs, Royal Irish Academy
Valerie Dowling, Senior Photographer, National Museum of Ireland
Clodagh Doyle, Assistant Keeper, Irish Folklife Division, National Museum of Ireland
Franz Fisher, Principal Researcher, St Patrick's *Confessio* Hypertext Stack Project, Royal Irish Academy
Jennifer Goff, Assistant Keeper, Art and Industrial Division, National Museum of Ireland
Andy Halpin, Assistant Keeper, Irish Antiquities Division, National Museum of Ireland

Sandra Heise, Assistant Keeper, Art and Industrial Division, National Museum of Ireland

Lar Joye, Assistant Keeper, Art and Industrial Division, National Museum of Ireland

Anne Keenan, Digital Image Technician, National Museum of Ireland

Éamonn Kelly, Keeper of Irish Antiquities, National Museum of Ireland

Andrea Kennedy, Account Manager, JPR Belfast

Christina Kennedy, Senior Curator: Head of Collections, Irish Museum of Modern Art

Michael Kenny, former Keeper of Art and Industry, National Museum of Ireland

Adrian Kerr, Manager, Museum of Free Derry

Brian Lacey, former Chief Executive, Discovery Programme

Séamas Mac Philib, Assistant Keeper, Irish Folklife Division, National Museum of Ireland

Eamonn McEneaney, Director, Waterford Museum of Treasures

Jim McGreevy, Director of Collections and Interpretation, National Museums Northern Ireland

Niall E. McKeith, Curator, National Science Museum at Maynooth

Bernard Meehan, Keeper of Manuscripts, Trinity College Dublin

Rosa Meehan, Assistant Keeper, Irish Folklife Division, National Museum of Ireland

Cameron Moffett, Curator (Collections), West Territory, English Heritage

Peter Moloney, Photographer

Dermot Mulligan, Curator, Carlow County Museum

Conor Newman, Senior Lecturer, Department of Archaeology, National University of Ireland, Galway

Raghnall Ó Floinn, Head of Collections, National Museum of Ireland

Jane Ohlmeyer, Erasmus Smith's Professor of Modern History, Trinity College Dublin

Michael Ruane, Pre-media Manager, The Irish Times

Bryan Rutledge, Photographer

Petra Schnabel, Assistant Librarian, Royal Irish Academy

Damian Shiels, Director, Rubicon Heritage Archaeological Services

Ronán Swan, Head of Archaeology, National Roads Authority

John Waddell, Emeritus Professor of Archaeology, National University of Ireland, Galway

Patrick F. Wallace, Former Director, National Museum of Ireland

Brian Walsh, Curator, County Museum Dundalk

Alex Ward, Assistant Keeper, Art and Industrial Division, National Museum of Ireland

Matt Wheeler, Curator/Manager, Irish Agricultural Museum

Audrey Whitty, Assistant Keeper, Art and Industrial Division, National Museum of Ireland

Thanks are also due to the anonymous reviewers for the Royal Irish Academy, for their views and suggestions, many of which have been quietly incorporated.

The other institutions centrally involved in this project are *The Irish Times* and the Royal Irish Academy. At *The Irish Times*, I would especially like to thank Geraldine Kennedy, Kevin O'Sullivan, Liam Kavanagh, Gerry Smyth, Conor Goodman, Lynda O'Keeffe, Liam Stebbing and Joyce Hickey. With the RIA, I have been fortunate to have fallen among the superb production team of Ruth Hegarty, Helena King and Fidelma Slattery, who have shown patience, ingenuity and professionalism beyond the bounds of normal endurance.

1. Mesolithic fish trap: **National Roads Authority**. Photography by John Sunderland

2. Ceremonial axehead, 3. Neolithic bowl, 4. Fint macehead, 5. Neolithic bag, 6. Basket earrings, 7. Pair of gold discs, 8. Coggalbeg gold hoard, 9. Bronze Age funerary pots, 10. Tara torcs, 11. Mooghaun hoard, 12. Gleninsheen gold gorget, 13. Castlederg bronze cauldron, 14. Iron spearhead, 15. Broighter boat, 16. Armlet, Old-croghan man, 17. Loughnashade trumpet, 18. Keshcarrigan bowl, 19. Corleck head, 20. Petrie 'Crown', 23. Mullaghmast stone, 24. St Patrick's bell, 25. Springmount wax tablets, 26. Ballinderry brooch, 27. Donore handle, 29. 'Tara' brooch, 30. Ardagh chalice, 31. Derrynaflan paten, 32. Moylough belt shrine, 33. Rinnagan crucifixion plaque, 36. Ballinderry sword, 37. Decorated lead weights, 38. Roscrea brooch, 39. Slave chain, 40. Silver cone, 41. Carved crook, 42. Breac Maodhóg, 43. Clonmacnoise crozier, 44. Cross of Cong, 47. Figure of a horseman, 48. Domhnach Airgid, 50. Two coins, 51. Processional cross, 53. De Burgo-O'Malley chalice, 54. Kavanagh charter horn, 58. Morion, 62. O'Queely chalice, 63. Fleetwood cabinet, 65. King William's gauntlets, 66. Crucifixion stone, 68. Wood's halfpence, 69. Dillon regimental flag, 70. Rococo silver candlestick, 72. Cotton panel with Volunteer review, 73. Pike, 75. Penrose glass decanter, 76. Robert Emmet's ring, 77. Wicker cradle, 78. Daniel O'Connell's 'chariot', 79. Stokes 'tapestry', 81. Six-gallon cooking pot, 82. Emigrant's teapot, 83. William Smith O'Brien gold cup, 84. Parnell silver casket, 86. Youghal lace collar, 87. GAA medal, 88. Reclining Buddha, 90. Lamp from *River Clyde*, 91. James Connolly's shirt, 92. Rejected coin design, 93. Boyne coracle, 94. Eileen Gray chair, 95. Emigrant's suitcase, 100. Decommissioned AK47: **National Museum of Ireland**. Photography by Valerie Dowling, Peter Moloney, Bryan Rutledge; image optimisation by Anne Keenan.

21. Cunorix stone: **English Heritage**. Photograpy by Paul Highnam.

22. St. Patrick's *Confessio,* Book of Armagh, TCD MS52_22r, 28. *Book of Kells,* TCD MS58_99v, 114v, 124r; 61. Deposition on Atrocities, 1641, TCD MS840_027r: **Trinity College Dublin Library**.

34. Tall cross, Monasterboice: **National Monuments Service**, Photographic Unit.

35. Oseberg Ship: **Kulturhistorisk museum, Universitetet i Oslo** (Museum of Cultural History, University of Oslo, Norway). Photography by Eirik Irgens Johnsen.

45. 'Strongbow's tomb': **Christ Church Cathedral, Dublin**. Photography by Cyril Byrne.

46. Giraldus Cambrensis Ms 700 f.75v – *Laudabiliter* (photography by Irish Script on Screen), 59. Site of *Leac na Ríogh*, Richard Bartlett map of Tullaghogue, Co. Tyrone, Ms2656, illustration reproduced from RIA copy of G.A. Hayes McCoy (ed.), 1964 *Ulster and other Irish maps c.1600* Dublin, Stationery Office for the Irish Manuscripts Commission, p. 11, 74. Act of Union blacklist, Ms 5696, 80. Captain Rock threatening letter, Ms 7519: **National Library of Ireland.**

49. Waterford Charter Roll, 52. Magi Cope: **Waterford Museum of Treasures.** Photography by Simon Hill, Scirebröc/Gamma Photos (49) and Terry Murphy Media (52).

55. Gallowglass gravestone replica: **GAA Museum, Croke Park**. Photography by David Sleator.

56. Book of Common Prayer: **Royal Irish Academy.**

57. Salamander pendant, 60. Wassail bowl, 71. Engraving of linen-makers, *Ulster Museum Collection*. 67. Conestoga Wagon *Ulster American Folk Park Collection. 89. Titanic* launch ticket. *Ulster Folk and Transport Museum Collection*: **National Museums Northern Ireland**

64. Book of Survey and Distribution, Co. Meath and Down Survey Baronial Map, Barony of Duleek, Co. Meath: **National Archives of Ireland.**

85. Carlow Cathedral pulpit (Pic.2: St Patrick meeting with King Laoghaire at Tara explaining his fire on the Hill of Slane, which is in the background of the panel. Pic.3: St Laserian, one of three carved figures who stand at the base of the pulpit, is the patron of the Diocese of Leighlin. In the middle is St Patrick's Angel Victor and the third is St Conleth, the patron of the Diocese of Kildare): **Carlow County Museum.**

93. Sketch of 'The curach' reproduced from RIA copy of William F. Wakeman, 1891 *Archaeologica Hibernica: a hand-book of Irish antiquities, pagan and Christian* (2nd edn; originally published 1848), Dublin and London, p. 263.

96. Washing machine: **Irish Agicultural Museum**. Photography by Patrick Browne.

97. Bloody Sunday handkerchief: **Mirrorpix.**

98. Intel Microprocessor chip: **Intel Ireland.**

99. Anglo-Irish Bank sign: **Getty Images.**

Jonathan Bardon 1982 *Belfast: an illustrated history*. Belfast. Blackstaff Press.

Jonathan Bardon 1992 *A history of Ulster*. Chester Springs, PA. Dufour Editions.

T.C. Barnard 2005 *A guide to the sources for the history of material culture in Ireland, 1500–2000*. Dublin. Four Courts.

Jonah Barrington 1809 *Historic anecdotes and secret memoirs of the legislative union between Great Britain and Ireland*. London. G. Robinson.

Jonathan Bell and Mervyn Watson 2008 *A history of Irish farming 1750–1950*. Dublin. Four Courts.

Walter Benjamin 1968 *Illuminations: essays and reflections*. New York. Houghton Mifflin Harcourt.

Eileen Black (ed.) 1991 *Ulster Museum: catalogue of the permanent collection*. Belfast. Ulster Museum.

William Carleton 1881 'Wildgoose Lodge', in *The works of William Carleton* (3 vols, vol. 3), 936–44. New York.

Jude Collins 2012 *Whose past is it anyway: the Easter Rising, the Ulster Covenant and the Battle of the Somme*. Dublin. History Press.

Commissioners of Irish Poor Enquiry 1835 *Poor inquiry—(Ireland): report on the state of the Irish poor in Great Britain*. London. HMSO.

James Cranford 1642 *The teares of Ireland*. London. A.N. for John Rothwell.

Bernadette Cunningham and Siobhán Fitzpatrick (eds) 2009 *Treasures of the Royal Irish Academy Library*. Dublin. Royal Irish Academy.

Thomas D'Arcy McGee 1852 *A history of the Irish settlers in North America: from the earliest period to the Census of 1850*. Boston. Patrick Donahoe.

Gustave de Beaumont 1839 *L'Irlande: sociale, politique e religeuse* (Ireland: social, political and religious). Paris. Michel Lévy Frère.

Herbert Davis (ed.) 1935 *The Drapier's letters to the people of Ireland against receiving Wood's Halfpence by Jonathan Swift*. Oxford. Clarendon Press.

I. Delamere and C. O'Brien 2005 *500 years of Irish silver*. National Museum of Ireland Monograph Series, 1. Dublin. National Museum of Ireland.

Robert James Dickson 1966 *Ulster emigration to Colonial America 1718–1775*. Belfast. Ulster Historical Foundation.

C. Doyle *et al.* 2007 *Guide to the National Museum of Ireland—Country Life*. Dublin. National Museum of Ireland.

Mairead Dunlevy 1999 *Dress in Ireland*. Cork. Collins Press.

N.M. Dunlevy, Michael Kenny and S. McElroy 2007 *Guide to the National Museum of Ireland—Collins Barracks*. Dublin. National Museum of Ireland.

Robert Emmet 1922 *Speech from the dock: Delivered at the Sessions House, Dublin, before Lord Norbury, on being found guilty of high treason as leader of the insurrection of 1803*. Dublin. Free Press Printery.

Emyr Estyn Evans 1957 *Irish folk ways*. London. Routledge and Keegan Paul. (Reprinted 2000; London. Dover Publications.)

R.F. Foster 2011 *Charles Stewart Parnell: the man and his family*. London. Faber and Faber.

Peter Fox (ed.) 1986 *Treasures of the Library, Trinity College, Dublin*. Dublin. Royal Irish Academy for the Library of Trinity College Dublin.

Edward Augustus Freeman 2010 *A short history of the Norman conquest of England*. Charleston, SC. BiblioBazaar. (Reprint; first published 1880, Oxford, Clarendon Press.)

Brian Friel 1990 'Dancing at Lughnasa: a play'. London. Faber.

Patrick M. Geoghegan 2002 *Robert Emmet: a life*. Dublin. Gill and Macmillan.

John M. Hearne (ed) 2010 *Glassmaking in Ireland. From the medieval to the contemporary*. Dublin. Irish Academic Press.

Michael W. Herren 1974 *The Hisperica Famina: a new critical edition with English translation and philological commentary*. Toronto. Pontifical Institute of Medieval Studies.

Joe Hogan 2001 *Basketmaking in Ireland*. Bray. Wordwell.

Francis J.H. Jenkinson 2012 *The Hisperica Famina: edited with a short introduction and index verborum*. Cambridge. Cambridge University Press. (Reprint; originally published 1908.)

James Joyce 1922 *Ulysses*. Paris. Sylvia Beach.

Juvenal c. first–second century AD *Satires* (Book 2). A translation by Lewis Evans of *The satires of Juvenal, Persius, Sulpicia and Lucilius* was published in 1860 in London by Henry G. Bohn.

Éamonn P. Kelly and Maeve Sikora 2011 *The Treasury. A guide to the exhibition*. Dublin. National Museum of Ireland.

Michael Kenny 1993 *The road to freedom*. Dublin. Townhouse.

Michael Kenny 1994 *The Fenians*. Dublin. Townhouse.

Michael Kenny 1996 *The 1798 Rebellion*. Dublin. Townhouse.

Rudyard Kipling 1914 *Kim*. New York. Doubleday.

Noel Kissane 1994 *Treasures from the National Library of Ireland*. Drogheda. National Library of Ireland.

Pádraig Lenihan 2003 *1690: Battle of the Boyne*. Stroud. Tempus Publishing.

Seán Mac Airt and Gearóid Mac Niocaill (eds) 1983 *The annals of Ulster (to AD 1131): text and translation*. Dublin. Dublin Institute for Advanced Studies.

Críostóir Mac Cárthaigh (ed.) 2008 *The traditional boats of Ireland*. Cork. Collins Press.

Oliver MacDonagh 2003 *Ireland: the Union and its aftermath*. Dublin. UCD Press. (Reprint; originally published 1977.)

J.P. Maclear 1911 *Sailing directions for Iceland, Greenland Sea, Spitzbergen, and the East Coast of Greenland* (2nd edn). *Originally compiled from various sources by Vice-admiral J P. Maclear*. London. J.D. Potter.

Máire Mac Neill 1962 *The festival of Lughnasa: a study of the survival of the Celtic festival of the beginning of harvest* (2 vols). Dublin. Irish Folklore Commission.

Thomas MacNevin 1845 *The history of the Volunteers of 1782* (4th edn). Dublin. James Duffy.

Alexander McBain 1917 *Celtic mythology and religion*. London. Oracle Books.

Eamonn McEneaney and R. Ryan (eds) 2004 *Waterford treasures*. Waterford. Waterford Museum of Treasures.

Mark McLaughlin 1980 *The Wild Geese: the Irish Brigades of France and Spain*. Oxford. Osprey Publishing.

J.P. Mallory 2013 *The Origins of the Irish*. London. Thames and Hudson.

Thomas A. Malthus 1807 *An essay on the principle of population; or a view of its past and present effects on human happiness; with an enquiry into our prospects respecting the future removal or mitigation of the evils which it occasions*. London. T. Bensley.

Ammianus Marcellinus c. fourth century AD *The roman history of Ammianus Marcellinus: during the reigns of the emperors Constantius, Julian, Jovianus, Valentinian and Valens*. A translation by C.D. Yonge was published in 1862 in London by Henry G. Bohn.

John Masefield 1916 *Gallipoli*. London. Macmillan.

Bernard Meehan 2012 *The Book of Kells*. London. Thames and Hudson.

Hiram Morgan 1993 *Tyrone's rebellion: the outbreak of the Nine Years War in Tudor Ireland*. London. Royal Historical Society.

Eibhlín Dubh Ní Chonaill 1971 *Caoineadh Airt Uí Laoghaire* (Lament for Art O'Leary). Dublin. Irish University Press.

Raghnall Ó Floinn 1994 *Irish shrines and reliquaries of the Middle Ages*. Dublin. Townhouse.

Raghnall Ó Floinn (ed) 2011 *Franciscan faith: sacred art in Ireland, AD 1600–1750*. National Museum of Ireland Monograph Series, 5. Dublin. National Museum of Ireland.

Claidhbh Ó Gibne 2012 *The Boyne currach*. Dublin. Open Air.

Dáithí Ó hÓgáin 1999 *The sacred isle: belief and religion in pre-Christian Ireland*. Woodbridge and Cork. Boydell Press and Collins Press.

Micheál Ó Siochrú 2008 *God's executioner: Oliver Cromwell and the conquest of Ireland*. London. Faber.

John Anthony O'Brien 1953 *The vanishing Irish: the enigma of the modern world*. Columbus, OH. McGraw Hill.

John O'Donovan (ed. and trs.) 1845–51 *Annála Rioghachta Eireann. Annals of the Kingdom of Ireland by the Four Masters, from the earliest period to the year 1616. Edited from MSS in the Library of the Royal Irish Academy and of Trinity College Dublin with a translation and copious notes* (7 vols). Dublin. Royal Irish Academy.

Jane H. Ohlmeyer (ed.) 1995 *Ireland from independence to occupation, 1641–1660*. Cambridge. Cambridge University Press.

Thomas Pakenham 1970 *The year of liberty: the story of the great Irish rebellion of 1798*. New Jersey. Prentice Hall.

Charles Plummer 1910 *Vitae Sanctorum Hiberniae: partim hactenus ineditae*. Oxford. Clarendon Press.

Muriel A.C. Press (trs.) 1899 *Laxdæla saga*. London. J.M. Dent. The translation is available as a free download via Project Gutenburg at: http://www.gutenberg.org/ebooks/17803 (25 November 2012).

Barry Raftery 1994 *Pagan Celtic Ireland: the enigma of the Irish Iron Age*. London. Thames and Hudson.

A.B. Scott and F.X. Martin (eds and trs) 1978) *Expugnation Hibernica: The Conquest of Ireland by Giraldus Cambrensis*. Dublin. Royal Irish Academy.

David and Sally Shaw-Smith 2003 *Traditional crafts of Ireland*. London. Thames and Hudson.

Robert Sloan 2000 *William Smith O'Brien and the Young Ireland Rebellion of 1848*. Dublin. Four Courts.

Peter Sheridan 1999 *44: Dublin made me*. New York. Viking.

Tacitus *c.* 98 CE *The life of Gnaeus Julius Agricola*. A translation by Alfred John Church and William Jackson Brodribb is available on Fordham University's Ancient History Sourcebook, at http://www.fordham.edu/halsall/ancient/tacitus-agricola.asp (25 November 2012).

John Teahan (ed.) 1990 *Irish decorative arts, 1550–1928*. Dublin. National Museum of Ireland.

John Teahan 1994 *Irish furniture and woodcraft*. Dublin. Townhouse.

John Waddell 2005. *The prehistoric archaeology of Ireland*. Bray. Wordwell.

P.F. Wallace and Valerie Dowling 2000 *A guide to the National Museum of Ireland*. Dublin. Townhouse.

P.F. Wallace and Raghnall Ó Floinn (eds) 2002 *Treasures of the National Museum of Ireland—Irish antiquities*. Dublin. Gill and Macmillan.

Robin Waterfield 2010 *Polybius, The histories: a new translation*. Oxford. Oxford University press.

Arthur Young 1780 *A tour In Ireland: with general observations on the present state of that kingdom*. London. Thomas Cadell.

Susan M. Youngs (ed) 1989 *'The work of angels': masterpieces of Celtic metalwork, 6th–9th centuries AD*. London. British Museum Press.

100

Oslo
35

55
Clonca
Graveyard,
Donegal
FREE ADMISSION

97
Museum of Free Derry,
Bloody Sunday Centre
ADMISSION CHARGES APPLY

Tullaghogue,
Tyrone
FREE ADMISSION

59

Ulster American
Folk Park, Omagh 67
ADMISSION CHARGES APPLY

Ulster Museum, Belfast. FREE ADMISSION 57 • 60 • 71

Ulster Folk & Transport Museum, Cultra 89
ADMISSION CHARGES APPLY

81 • 82 National Museum of Ireland –
93 • 95 Country Life, Castlebar, Mayo
FREE ADMISSION

Monasterboice, Louth 34
FREE ADMISSION

National Science Museum at Maynooth
FREE ADMISSION 98

DUBLIN
See detailed city
map opposite

Carlow County Museum 85
FREE ADMISSION

Irish Agricultural Museum, Wexford
ADMISSION CHARGES APPLY

UK
11 • 21

96

Waterford Museum of Treasures 49 • 52
ADMISSION CHARGES APPLY

Derrynane House, Caherdaniel, Kerry
78 ADMISSION CHARGES APPLY

DUBLIN

CROKE PARK

55 (H)

JONES'S RD
NORTH CIRCULAR RD
BALLYBOUGH RD
SUMMERHILL
PORTLAND ROW

50 • 53 • 58 • 62 • 63 • 65 • 66
68 • 69 • 70 • 72 • 73 • 75 • 76
77 • 79 • 83 • 84 • 86 • 87 • 88
90 • 91 • 92 • 94 • 99 • 100

PARNELL ST
O'CONNELL ST
TALBOT ST
HENRY ST
MARY ST
ABBEY ST

(A)

BENBURB ST
WOLFE TONE QY
ELLIS QY
ARRAN QY
BACHELORS WLK
VICTORIA QUAY
USHERS ISL
INNS QY
ORMOND QY UPR
ORMOND QY LWR
ASTON QY
USHERS QY
MERCHANTS QUAY
WELLINGTON QY

DAME ST

(G) 22 • 28 • 61
TRINITY
COLLEGE

HIGH ST
LORD EDWARD ST
NASSAU ST

(B)

45

STH GT GEORGES ST
GRAFTON ST
DAWSON ST
KILDARE ST

(F) 46 • 59 • 74 • 80
(E)

PATRICK ST
BRIDE ST
AUNGIER ST

(D)

56

1 • 2 • 3 • 4 • 5 • 6
7 • 8 • 9 • 10 • 11
12 • 13 • 14 • 15
16 • 17 • 18 • 19
20 • 23 • 24 • 25
26 • 27 • 29 • 30
31 • 32 • 33 • 36
37 • 38 • 39 • 40
41 • 42 • 43 • 44
47 • 48 • 51 • 54

(C)

64

KEVIN ST CUFFE ST

ST STEPHENS
GREEN

A
National Museum of Ireland–
Decorative Arts and History
Collins Barracks, Benburb Street, Dublin 7
FREE ADMISSION

B
Christ Church Cathedral
Christchurch Place, Dublin 8
ADMISSION CHARGES APPLY

C
National Archives of Ireland
Bishop Street, Dublin 8
FREE ADMISSION

D
Royal Irish Academy
19 Dawson Street, Dublin 2
FREE ADMISSION

E
National Museum of Ireland – Archaeology
Kildare Street, Dublin 2
FREE ADMISSION

F
National Library of Ireland
Kildare Street, Dublin 2
FREE ADMISSION

G
Trinity College – The Old Library
College Green, Dublin 2
ADMISSION CHARGES APPLY

H
GAA Museum
Croke Park, St Joseph's Avenue (off Clonliffe Road), Dublin 3
ADMISSION CHARGES APPLY

MY 100 OBJECTS TRAIL

Keep a record here of the objects you have visited. Collect a stamp from the front desk at the museums.
Consult www.100objects.ie for rewards offered when you use the trail.

1	2	3	4	5
6	7	8	9	10
11	12	13	14	15
16	17	18	19	20
21	22	23	24	25
26	27	28	29	30
31	32	33	34	35
36	37	38	39	40
41	42	43	44	45

| 46 | 47 | 48 | 49 | 50 |

| 51 | 52 | 53 | 54 | 55 |

| 56 | 57 | 58 | 59 | 60 |

| 61 | 62 | 63 | 64 | 65 |

| 66 | 67 | 68 | 69 | 70 |

| 71 | 72 | 73 | 74 | 75 |

| 76 | 77 | 78 | 79 | 80 |

| 81 | 82 | 83 | 84 | 85 |

| 86 | 87 | 88 | 89 | 90 |

| 91 | 92 | 93 | 94 | 95 |

| 96 | 97 | 98 | 99 | 100 |

234